"Ryan's book brought me on a heartfelt journey through Singapore's vibrant hawker culture, evoking a profound sense of pride in our culinary heritage. He has beautifully captured the resilience and enterprising spirit of the hawkers, whose dedication provides Singaporeans with delicious, affordable meals every day. This celebration of our unique food culture is a testament to the rich tapestry of traditions and flavours that characterise our nation."

Mdm Halimah Yacob
Chancellor, Singapore University of Social Sciences
Former President of Singapore

"Hawker centres are a distinctive feature of Singapore's urban landscape. They are community spaces where people from all walks of life take their meals, meet family and friends, and enjoy a great variety of culinary delights from our multi-ethnic cultures. That Singapore was recently awarded UNESCO's Representative List of the Intangible Cultural Heritage of Humanity speaks to the uniqueness and significance of our hawker culture. What started as an economic activity that catered to the needs of transient populations and provided employment to the urban poor, became an integral part of the post-independent government's early policies of industrialisation, urban renewal and preservation of communal spaces for social interaction among the different races. The author attempts to trace the evolution of hawking from pre-colonial Singapore to contemporary times with the incipient emergence of a new generation of artisan hawkers. How this 'gentrification' of the hawker culture will pan out and help to safeguard the heritage remains to be seen. This book stirs our interest and concern over a changing socio-cultural facet of life in Singapore which has become a part of the Singaporean identity itself."

Dr Aline Wong
Sociologist
Former Senior Minister of State for Health and Education

"I love this book. As a champion of our hawkers and a lover of hawker food, this book tells the often-forgotten story of how hawker centres came to be. I am happy to commend the book."

Professor Tommy Koh
Ambassador-At-Large at the Ministry of Foreign Affairs

"A fascinating read! This book tells a compelling story of the humble beginning of hawker centres and hawker fare, and how they have evolved into the multi-ethnic and multi-cultural hawker culture in Singapore. It is a valuable resource for food diplomacy in promoting Singapore's uniqueness and multiculturalism."

Peter Tan
Singapore's Ambassador to the People's Republic of China

"An outstanding history of how Singapore turned a common hawking problem into a unique social engineering phenomenon, this study not only shows us how effective governance can ensure progress, but also alerts us to the continual pressures to adapt and change."

Wang Gungwu
National University of Singapore

*"*From Streets to Stalls: The History and Evolution of Hawking and Hawker Centres in Singapore *by Ryan Kueh comes on the heels of a range of books about Singapore's hawker centres. It is especially welcome because the author represents the younger generation which is sometimes thought to be disinterested in hawker centres. Ryan Kueh has successfully turned his undergraduate project into an accessible book for the general public,*

providing insights into the history of hawker centres, from the 19ᵗʰ century to the present. A welcome addition to the literature.”

Professor Lily Kong
President
Singapore Management University

"Ryan Kueh is a distinguished alumnus of Tsinghua University's Schwarzman College who has always impressed me with his observations and insights of social phenomena. For Singaporeans, hawker centres are 'community canteens' that serve local fare at affordable prices. For foreign travellers, hawker centres are a must-go place to experience authentic Singaporean culture. For administrators, hawker centres are an example of how one can learn the knowhow of managing the once-scattered street food vendors. Regardless of your profession, anyone from every background can find a relatable chapter.”

David Pan
Executive Dean and Professor
Schwarzman College, Tsinghua University

"In the total urban transformation of the island, the hawker centre has emerged as an essential social institution in Singaporean everyday life. In documenting a history of the reorganisation of the free-floating itinerant hawkers into a purpose-built centre and, its evolution into an intangible international heritage, this book provides us with deeper knowledge of a constitutive piece of the overall urban fabric.”

Chua Beng Huat
Emeritus Professor
National University of Singapore

From Streets *to* Stalls

The History and Evolution
of Hawking and Hawker
Centres in Singapore

From Streets *to* Stalls

The History and Evolution
of Hawking and Hawker
Centres in Singapore

Ryan Kueh

World Scientific

NEW JERSEY · LONDON · SINGAPORE · BEIJING · SHANGHAI · HONG KONG · TAIPEI · CHENNAI · TOKYO

Published by

World Scientific Publishing Co. Pte. Ltd.

5 Toh Tuck Link, Singapore 596224

USA office: 27 Warren Street, Suite 401-402, Hackensack, NJ 07601

UK office: 57 Shelton Street, Covent Garden, London WC2H 9HE

National Library Board, Singapore Cataloguing in Publication Data
Name(s): Kueh, Ryan.
Title: From streets to stalls : the history and evolution of hawking and
    hawker centres in Singapore / Ryan Kueh.
Description: Singapore : World Scientific Publishing Co. Pte. Ltd., 2024.
Identifier(s): ISBN 978-981-12-9353-5 (hardback) | 978-981-12-9438-9 (paperback) |
    978-981-12-9354-2 (ebook for institutions) | 978-981-12-9355-9 (ebook for individuals)
Subject(s): LCSH: Street vendors--Singapore--History. | Peddling--Singapore--History. |
    Food courts--Singapore.
Classification: DDC 381.18095957 --dc23

British Library Cataloguing-in-Publication Data
A catalogue record for this book is available from the British Library.

The painting on the cover, titled "Hougang Hainanese Village (後港海南椰園村)", was illustrated by
Yip Yew Chong in 2021. The mural is owned by the Serangoon Khiung Jai Co-Villagers Association.

For any available supplementary material, please visit
https://www.worldscientific.com/worldscibooks/10.1142/13849#t=suppl

Desk Editor: Jiang Yulin
Sub-editor: Claudia Tan Kexin

Typeset by Stallion Press
Email: enquiries@stallionpress.com

About the Author

Ryan Kueh is a Singaporean who is passionate about the intersection of consumption culture and history. He holds a master's degree from Tsinghua University under the Schwarzman Scholars programme and completed his bachelor's at Yale-NUS College, reading Politics, Philosophy, Economics (PPE) and History.

For his next passion project, Ryan is researching the evolution of Singaporean Chinese/Nanyang Chinese cuisine. Specifically, he aims to uncover why and how local delicacies have evolved vis-à-vis their Chinese origins, unpacking the idiosyncrasies and uniqueness of local culture.

Contents

ΙΟΙ

Foreword

The hawker tradition is deeply embedded in the fabric of Singapore's history and culture. It is a story of enterprise, resilience, adaptation, and community. From its beginnings in the 19th century, hawking has consistently featured as a source of affordable food for many Singaporeans. It was a time when street vendors peddled their goods to customers, embodying the entrepreneurial spirit that thrived in the bustling port city. Yet, this popular industry was not without its challenges. With no formal regulations in place, hawkers faced constant struggles against overcrowding, unsanitary conditions, and economic uncertainty. However, out of these challenges emerged a spirit of resilience and adaptability that would come to define the hawker culture in Singapore. Through sheer determination and ingenuity, hawkers found ways to innovate their trade, evolved their dishes and culinary techniques that would captivate the taste buds and served the needs of a growing population. It was this spirit of innovation that laid the foundation for the transformation of hawking into a cornerstone of Singaporean identity. As the years passed and Singapore continued to evolve, so too did its hawker culture. The establishment of hawker centres in the 1970s marked a significant turning point, providing locations for hawkers to operate in a more regulated and hygienic environment. These hawker centres quickly became more than just places to grab a quick and affordable meal — they became iconic symbols of Singaporean cosmopolitanism, where people from all walks of life could come together to savour the diverse flavours of the nation.

This important study by Ryan Kueh reminds us of the roots from which this vibrant hawker culture sprang. Through the pages of this book, the reader is treated to a compelling story, embedded in the rich historical tapestry of Singapore's social and urban history. This well-researched study documents the history and development of the hawker trade and hawking as a social phenomenon from the laissez-faire situation of a 19th century colony to the controlled environment created by a post-colonial state in the 1970s and 1980s. *From Streets to Stalls* shows how hawkers adapted and persisted as they faced the rapid changes that accompanied Singapore's transformation from colony to nation-state. Through this fascinating narrative, we are reminded of the invaluable contributions of generations of hawkers who have shaped the culinary and social landscape of Singapore, and whose legacy continues to define our identity today.

Ryan has worked on this project for several years with passion and commitment. I was Ryan's research advisor at Yale-NUS College from 2021 to 2023 and am happy to have played a small role in seeding the ideas for this book. It was an enjoyable exploration of Singapore's hawker history and culture for me, and I am delighted that the publication of this important study will now make it accessible to a wider audience. I am confident readers will find this book a captivating, informative study and an enjoyable read.

Tan Tai Yong
President, Singapore University of Social Sciences
Former President, Yale-NUS College
June 2024

Acknowledgements

This book has been long in the making, from its first inception as a student research project to an undergraduate capstone, to one that has grown into a multifaceted study of the specifics of Singapore's hawking history. As the saying goes, it takes a village to raise a child, and this book could not have been completed without the help of others. As such, I must acknowledge the contributors to this book — people who have given through both material and immaterial forms. This book would not have been possible without family, friends and mentors who have contributed in some shape or another.

First and most important of all, my biggest thanks goes to my partner, Claudia Tan. As my first, second and third reader, and as someone unfamiliar with the depths or nuances of Singapore's history, you were the guinea pig for all of the book's infant experiments. Yet, you approached my naïve tropes with openness and constructiveness. Your language acumen and novel insights have polished the book beyond what I could have ever done alone. For this, the readers of this book and I will be eternally grateful.

To the educators and peers from Yale-NUS College. Professor Tan Tai Yong, who saw this project from infancy to maturity. This appreciation extends to other educators who have contributed to the story through their teaching and matured my thinking and writing. This includes Associate Professor Emanuel Mayer, Associate Professor Chin-Hao Huang, Assistant Professor Steven Oliver and Dr Bjorn Gomes. Many thanks also to friends from Yale-NUS College (Ng Kye Been, Brendan Ng and Nicholas Choong) who had a part in refining earlier versions of this work.

Next, to the others who have made this possible. To the book's publisher, World Scientific, thank you for taking the chance on me. To Yip Yew Chong, thank you for contributing to the cover. I, alongside many other Singaporeans, greatly connect with your art. It is extraordinarily meaningful to have one of your murals fronting this book. Special mention goes to the officers at the National Archives of Singapore, the National Museum of Singapore and the National Heritage Board. I would also like to thank my mentors from Tsinghua University and the Singapore Embassy of Beijing, for making my time in China feel like a home away from home in the years 2023–2024.

Lastly, to all my family and friends, for their support in ensuring that I was always in the right headspace to engage in this tumultuous project. This includes friends from the Schwarzman Scholars programme, who are some of the best and brightest individuals I have met. Buddies such as Girish Menon and others from Yale-NUS College. Most important of all, the chieftains of the village include Mom, Dad, and my dearest brother, Justin Kueh, who is one of my role models and one of the biggest supporter of any ideas I have championed.

Chapter 1
Introduction

For most Singaporeans, hawker centres are an integral part of our daily routine. Be it breakfast, lunch or dinner, the hawker centre is our go-to for all things food. It is noisy and bustling, and its patrons will almost certainly sweat. Often, we face decision paralysis given the sheer number of options present. From Cantonese century egg porridge to Malay *nasi padang* to Indian *roti*, the choices are endless — and so are the queues.

In recent times, Singapore's hawker culture has gone global. Visiting hawker centres is an autochthonous ritual that Singaporeans experience daily and want others to experience as well, and hawker centres are now some of our key tourist attractions. We have done this so well that in 2020, Singapore's hawker culture was recognised as an 'Intangible Cultural Heritage of Humanity' by the United Nations Educational, Scientific and Cultural Organisation (UNESCO), representing "a living heritage shared by those who prepare hawker food and those who dine and mingle over hawker food in community dining spaces called hawker centres."[1]

But what really is a hawker centre? For many others around the world, hawker centres are a foreign concept. Centralised multi-storey centres containing an assortment of street food vendors with public dining facilities such as fixed chairs and tables are not a common feature in most countries, even if these countries possess significant street food vendor populations. Hawker centres are government-built, regulated shelters for hawkers to operate out of. The hawker centre's primary utility comes from its provision of order, mandating social mores of hygiene, spatial agglomeration and facilitating regulatory enforcement.

The hawker centre is distinctive in its embodied functions and social practices — or 'culture'. It is easy to conflate 'hawker culture' and street food culture, but once explicated, the distinctions are clear. Although hawking and street food cultures exist worldwide, Singapore's hawker culture is unique as it is a culmination of street food culture performed through the medium of the hawker centre. In essence, hawker centres are the spaces in which hawker culture is performed. This goes farther, for the hawker centre itself is a conduit for many other social and political forces. Socially, the hawker centre exists as a central 'third space',[2] a key gathering hub for social bonding and cohesion over good and affordable food. Politically, the hawker centre exists as an instrument for the government to distribute welfare indirectly to citizens by means of affordable food, and as one of the vehicles through which Singapore's policy of multiculturalism plays out.

Although modern hawker culture is closely intertwined with the hawker centre, this has not always been the case. Hawker centres — distinct from hawker shelters (more on this in later chapters) — are a relatively recent phenomenon, only coming into existence in the early 1970s. Before hawker centres, hawker culture in Singapore was reminiscent of street food culture across the world, characterised by independent and itinerant hawkers who hawked simple fare on the streets. They were challenging to regulate, being not only numerous but disorderly, unhygienic and uncooperative in their operations. Vendors would hawk on the sidewalk and dispose of food waste improperly, attracting vermin and pests. Hawkers would congregate around central districts, blocking key streets and congesting roads. Hawkers come in all shapes and forms, from simple basket hawkers to more substantive versions such as pushcart vendors, commonly found in the streets of Malaysia or Thailand. Internationally, there are the *yatais* in Japan, pushcarts in New York and Los Angeles, and the *warungs* (kiosks) in Indonesia.

In response to such challenges, there are two main modes of recourse for governments. The first is through prosecution — such as fining illegal hawkers or chasing them off the streets — a symptomatic mode of action mostly undertaken by developing countries. With a weak state and poor economic conditions, developing countries often do not have the resources to permanently deal with vast numbers of illegal itinerant hawkers. Attempts to address this issue are piecemeal, as law enforcement only punishes illegal hawkers as and when they can. Such a solution is only temporary, with hawkers returning after law enforcement leave.

The second way is through eradication, a course of action mostly undertaken by developed countries. Eradication is performed in two ways: First, by way of prosecution, where hawkers are banned outright or heavily controlled; second, through permanent economic uplifting, where hawkers are redirected to better and more stable jobs. Given the presence of better economic opportunities and heavy regulation, developed countries often have a low number of hawkers or street food vendors. This is easily exemplified by the difference in the street food scene between Europe and Asia.

Modern Singapore sits at a unique interstice, a developed country with a relatively high number of hawkers in its system selling affordable food. It is one of the few countries to have successfully regulated and reduced its hawker population without substantively losing the trade or its cultural or social utilities. Whilst other street food forms are typically characterised by their informality and lack of regulation, Singapore's hawker culture differs in its formalisation and discipline of the industry. Singapore has solved the so-called 'hawker problem', permanently addressing common hawker-related issues of illegality, congestion, health and safety risks and fiscal evasion whilst retaining the benefits of the trade. This begs some big questions: How did Singapore control the rampant illegal hawker population and ameliorate hawker-related issues? What was the history of this development, and did hawkers play other roles in Singapore's history? How did hawker centres change this? This book seeks to answer these questions. In short, this is a book on the history of hawking and hawker centres. It is about the story of hawking and the relationships surrounding hawking, and how these have changed over time.

Before we begin, I want to share three primary motivations for undertaking this extensive project. The first motivation is a historical one. Within this book, I seek to uncover the origins and evolutions of hawking within Singapore. This inquiry takes us back to pre-colonial 'Singapore', with Chapter 3 exploring whether hawkers existed around ninth and 14th century Singapore through archaeological and literary evidence. Chapters 4 and 5 expound on hawker culture before independence from 1819 to 1965. Then, hawking was mostly itinerant and illegal, with hawkers rampant on the streets, posing problems for public order and national development. Chapters 6 and 7 cover the reform of the hawker trade (hawker reform), defined in this book as the period from 1969 to 1973. Chapter 6 explores the motivating drivers (*the why*) behind the reform. It touches on the political impact of hawkers, where hawkers were a labour group that challenged the state for territory and rent. They also deprived the state of labour during Singapore's economic reform in the late 1960s and 1970s. Chapter 7 explores the mechanisms and execution (*the how*) of the hawker reform, touching on the specific instruments used to substantively enforce hawker policy, which in the process fundamentally reshaped the hawking scene into what it is today.

The second motivation is a sociological one: I hope to dig deeper into hawking as a cultural and social phenomenon. Chapter 8 touches on the specific cultural changes ushered in by the hawker centre. During the colonial era, hawking was privately initiated, disorganised and informal. It was also largely dominated by Chinese and Indian immigrants. After independence, with the advent of hawker centres, hawking became formalised, sanitised and orderly, with the trade ethnically rebalanced. We will also discuss how hawker centres became key spaces for Singapore's multicultural policies to manifest. Lastly,

Chapter 9 outlines some continuities and changes in hawking's sociocultural importance. Hawkers were, and continue to be, an important source of affordable food, and the trade has helped people remain in gainful employment. This social utility has remained despite drastic changes to Singapore's economy, with hawking becoming an integral vehicle for the state's wider social policies. Further, it touches on how hawkers are increasingly viewed as artisans, guardians of an increasingly forgotten heritage as the country propels itself forward.

The third and final motivation is a sentimental one. Hawkers tell the story and struggles of the layperson. They exemplify the hardships of the ordinary Singaporean through Singapore's most trying years, where older generations' forays into hawking were born out of necessity, undertaken in hopes of lifting the next generation out of adversity. This is why many Singaporeans have family members who used to be hawkers or are currently still hawkers themselves. My grandparents, too, were once hawkers, peddling Teochew fish soup at Serangoon Avenue in the 1980s. My father, an army regular at that time, recalls having to help out at my mother's (his then-girlfriend) parents' stall after booking out of camp each week. It proved to be an effective courting strategy, with my parents getting married a few years later.

For me, the story of my grandparents' hawker stall is emblematic of the representative power of hawking, reflective of what life was like during a certain period and how it has changed over time. As Singapore progressively entrenches itself in the developed world, hawking will continue to change. This also means its history, heritage and traditions are under threat of being lost to the haste of modernity. For my international readers, I hope this book provides some inspiration for how to see the development of hawking or street food vending differently. Through the successes and failures of extensive policy attempts in Singapore, Singapore's journey can perhaps be a model for what works and what does not. For my Singaporean readers, I hope this book will inspire a deeper appreciation of hawker culture, which I believe we take for granted. Hawkers, hawking and hawker centres are a living testament to the history, tenacity and changing identities of Singaporeans. They are places containing the aspirations of a 'new Singapore', seen through the likes of trendy, new hawker stalls. Conversely, they are also places that actively appreciate the past, a praxis of the various traditions that grounded Singapore through its formative years. Only by understanding the past and tracing the origins and history of hawking in Singapore, can we better understand what must be done to bring our cultural heritage into the future for generations to come.

Chapter 2
Some First Principles of Hawking

Before diving into the book, I would like to take a moment to outline some first principles guiding my discussion on hawking in Singapore. First, I will locate hawking as a global phenomenon, one with enabling conditions and features that hold across different countries and contexts. Second, I will delineate this book's methodological principles; specifically, the frameworks and historical documents used to uncover the history of the hawker problem in Singapore. As we will come to see, hawking as a global phenomenon is both general and particular. Hawking develops as a reaction to external circumstances but also becomes a phenomenon that influences its surrounding stakeholders. It is controlled by many microeconomic and macroeconomic factors within a country, ranging from the health of the economy and unemployment to the presence of transient travellers, creating concomitant social and political issues that governments are left to manage through public policy. In most cases, this leaves a policy trail — the bread and butter of this book's historical investigation and reconstruction.

Hawking (Street Vending) as a Phenomenon

Generally, the demand for eating out is largely driven by people being unable or unwilling to cook for themselves. This often arises from a lack of factors such as space, time, energy or the absence of a support structure to provide home-cooked meals. This can manifest in diverse scenarios, from transient visitors in a foreign land to migrant workers who have ventured alone to another country in search of economic opportunity, to ordinary households searching for an affordable meal outside. This creates demand for others to supply cooked meals, a role which is often filled by hawkers selling food, drinks and produce.

Hawking as a phenomenon is widespread across the world, particularly in developing economies.[1] The specific nomenclature is dependent on cultural and geographical nuances, with 'street vending' preferred outside of Asia and 'hawking' dominant in places like Singapore and Malaysia. Amongst the notable works in this field, Ray Bromley's *Street Vending and Public Policy: A Global Review* stands out as a significant text. Bromley defines hawking as either a temporary or permanent occupation, unfolding in public spaces where individuals sell food, goods or services.[2] Their activities are often marked by mobility, operating at various locations and hours with few fixed routines or patterns, and characterised by small-scale, labour-intensive operations typically managed by an individual or a single family.

In contrast, formal hawkers are organised by a centralised operator, with vendors selling their wares with regulatory approval. They tend to be licensed, taxpaying and (generally) in compliance with the myriad regulations imposed by the state. This commonly takes the form of markets held regularly at standardised times and locations, such as farmers' markets, flea markets and Christmas markets,[3] like the renowned night markets of Chatuchak or Ratchada in Bangkok, Thailand. In Singapore, formal hawkers are vendors who sell their wares at wet markets or hawker centres.

Most hawkers across the globe, however, operate informally, participating in a trade that is unregulated and unlicensed. These hawkers remain informal for two reasons. The first is due to a lack of hawker-specific legislation that seeks to formalise the sector. The second is due to the difficulty in regulating them, with governments lacking the administrative will and manpower to carry out enforcement. From the hawker's perspective, there is little incentive to abide by legislation as it incurs unnecessary risks and costs, especially if the regulations can be easily circumvented, or if hawking is being undertaken as a stop-gap vocation. As many hawkers are often illegal, they continuously challenge the state for public territory and economic rent. Governments, in turn, may attempt to gain control by limiting itinerant hawking or even banning the trade. As such, many hawking practices revolve around circumventing laws, reflecting the "processual nature of street vending as a practice situated between avoiding and complying with governmental interference".[4] Such resistance against formalisation can be understood through Asef Bayat's concept of *quiet encroachment*, which refers to the "silent, protracted, but pervasive advancement of the ordinary people on the propertied, powerful, or the public, in order to survive and improve their lives."[5]

Problems and Salience of Hawking

Informal hawkers present a host of associated challenges whilst remaining important for communities and economies at large. Common issues include congestion, health and safety risks, taxation issues and the sale of substandard products, particularly food prepared without adhering to proper hygiene practices. At the same time, the phenomenon of hawking (both formal and informal) has socioeconomic utility, providing affordable food to the masses and serving as a quasi-safety net, earning it public acceptance.

Generally, in urban communities, informal hawkers pose two main issues: public health risks and urban pollution issues. First, informal hawkers are often associated with the spread of public health diseases due to unhygienic practices. This may result from a lack of proper hygiene training, poor food safety regulation, or in other cases, the improper disposal of leftover food, which clogs public drainage systems. In many instances, hawkers utilise unsanitary water sources — for example, using a single source of stale water to wash dishes or prepare consumables — especially when selling beverages like fruit juices or food items like freshly-cut fruits. This increases the risk of foodborne or public health diseases, a risk that is potentially exacerbated if a population is not inoculated against common diseases such as typhoid and cholera. Second, informal hawkers are also linked to spatial or urban pollution issues. This is especially so with itinerant hawkers, who tend to cluster in high-traffic areas in large numbers, congesting pedestrian walkways and roads. As hawkers become more entrenched in certain locations over time, it becomes increasingly difficult for authorities to introduce or maintain urban planning integrity. These problems are especially pronounced in cities with limited enforcement capabilities, with authorities often stuck in a continuous cat-and-mouse game with itinerant hawkers. As most countries urbanise and become increasingly dense, these issues are only likely to worsen.

Despite the issues associated with informal hawking, both formal and informal hawking fulfil various socioeconomic functions for administrators and citizens. The relatively low barriers to entry present hawking as a 'self-help' entrepreneurial option for individuals in need of transitory employment or an alternative income source. This allows the trade to effectively serve as an informal social safety net, especially in the absence of comprehensive employment support or welfare systems, and particularly in times of poor economic conditions.[6] This view has been adopted by the Thai authorities, who have publicly acknowledged the value of regulating and sometimes even facilitating hawking activities, considering them effective tools for poverty alleviation and sources of cultural capital, particularly in the context of tourism.[7]

The impetus to enter hawking often stems from administrative inefficiencies and an absence of sound employment alternatives. This has often led to longstanding sociopolitical tensions between hawkers and the state. On one hand, the trade compensates for, even if only partially, the state's social and economic policy blind spots. On the other, it can bring forth a slew of challenges, including disruptions to public order, daily administrative hurdles, public health concerns, spatial disorder and fiscal evasion. As hawkers provide an important service to the working class and are often members of the working class themselves, attempts to eliminate or regulate hawkers are often perceived as a direct affront to the people, simultaneously threatening access to affordable food while penalising vendors for seeking to be self-reliant. This dynamic underscores the complex interplay between hawking, governance and public sentiment, a central theme in understanding the history and significance of hawkers.

Hawking as a National Concern

The prevalence of informal hawking serves as a rough barometer of a nation's economic well-being. Historically, hawkers represent the most visible segment of the informal economy, embodying the daily struggles of everyday folk. Sociologist Maureen Hays-Mitchell proposes that hawking is a response to adverse social, economic and political conditions, as individuals who struggle to make ends meet through conventional economic opportunities resort to 'last-resort' entrepreneurial avenues.[8] A 2006 report from a meeting of the International Labour Organization stated that for the public, policymakers and hawkers alike, "street vending and poverty are part of the same equation."[9] Thus, it is possible to employ hawker numbers as a proportion of overall population ('hawker population density') as an indirect proxy for gauging macroeconomic health. The correlation here is negative; the better a country's economic health, the lower its hawker population density.

We may observe this empirically, as developing cities display, on aggregate, higher hawker population densities than their developed counterparts. Within developing cities, hawker population densities often hover around the range of 1.5% to 2.5%. For example, India's 2014 Street Vendors Act estimates that "hawkers reasonably constitute 2.5% of the population of a city", with most hawkers operating illegally.[10] This density is similar

Figure 2.1.   Percentage of Hawkers to Population in Phases 1, 2 and 3 (1931 to 1978)

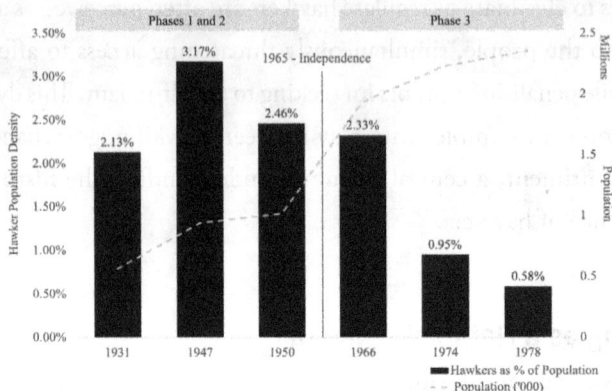

Note: Before 1966 Unlicensed, After 1966 Licensed.
Source: Ryan Kueh 2024. Compiled from Report of the Committee Appointed to Investigate the Hawker Question in Singapore 1931, 204–205; Straits Settlement Annual Report 1951, 73; Hawkers Inquiry Commission 1950, 68–69; Ministry of Environment/Hawkers Department (HD) Annual Report 1971–1973, 11; Ministry of Environment/Hawkers Department (HD) Statistics on Hawker Licences 1979, 2–3, 46, 53, 63, 120.

to Bangkok's, where there are an estimated 240,000 hawkers, or 2.36% of the population in 2018.[11] These figures are comparable to pre-independence Singapore; the city's hawker population density experienced a perceptible increase over two decades, going from 2.13% in 1931 to 2.46% in 1950 (see Figure 2.1). When compared to developed cities, there is a significant difference in the figures. In Los Angeles, some 50,000 street vendors make up approximately 1.26% of the population in 2019.[12] In post-hawker reform Singapore, hawker population density was substantially lower at 0.58% in 1978. This was achieved in Singapore after its independence in 1965, where, following swift and expansive economic reforms, hawker population density more than halved within a decade from 2.33% to 0.95% (1966 to 1974), and again in the following five years from 0.95% to 0.58% (1974 to 1978; see Figures 2.1 and 2.2). Hawker population density therefore emerges as an interesting barometer for measuring general economic development. Within the context of Singapore, efforts to address the issues of informal hawking were

Figure 2.2.   Hawkers as a Percentage of Population with GDP Growth (1966 to 1978)

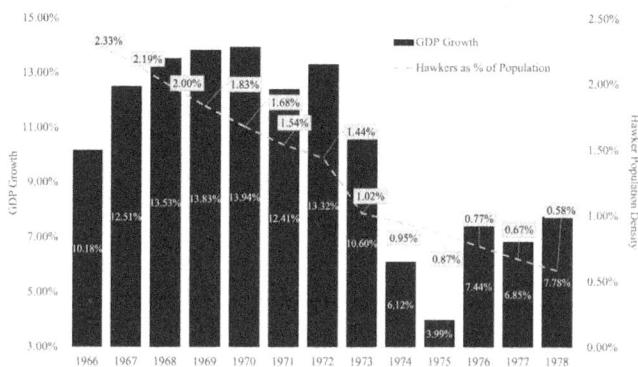

Source: Ryan Kueh 2024. Compiled from Straits Settlement Annual Report 1951, 73; Hawkers Inquiry Commission 1950, 68–69; Ministry of Environment/Hawkers Department (HD) Annual Report 1971–1973, 11; Ministry of Environment/Hawkers Department (HD) Statistics on Hawker Licences 1979, 2–3, 46, 53, 63, 120; World Bank, retrieved 2023; World Bank & OECD, retrieved 2023.

undergirded by a drive to reduce hawker population density instead of reducing or eliminating informal hawkers altogether.

Methodology

Despite the long-standing prevalence of hawking in Southeast Asia, historical research on motivations, enabling conditions and state policies governing hawkers is lacking. This book thus seeks to study hawking not only through a historical or sociological lens, but also from political and economic perspectives. Within this scope, we will trace the *longue durée* history of hawking in Singapore and uncover how the phenomenon grew vis-à-vis external political and economic events. The methodology relies on an extensive analysis of archival documents and modern literature, covering various administrations' approaches to tackling the 'hawker problem'. This includes analysing historical documents such as the Straits Settlement Blue Books, government commissions and Ministry annual reports, amongst others, and drawing on local academics to comprehensively understand the modern implications of hawking. The analysis focuses on itinerant and non-itinerant hawkers who sell cooked food, drinks and fruits. By way of a caveat, any hawker statistics reported before independence likely encompassed other types of hawkers, such as vendors of raw meat, fish, vegetables, dried goods and even textiles. This book's analysis is intentionally limited to food-based hawkers, as this helps us understand the development of hawker centres and how they played an important role in solving the 'hawker problem'.

Two frameworks can assist in this endeavour. The first is that of general hawking phases. The history of hawking in Singapore can be broadly categorised into three phases, each representing a different stage of evolution, as well as the respective administration's approach to solving the 'hawker problem':

- **Phase 1 (1819 to 1942): The origins of Singapore's modern hawkers and their associated issues.** This was during Singapore's early colonial era as the Straits Settlement Crown Colony.

- **Phase 2 (1942 to 1965): The growth of the hawker population in Singapore and exacerbation of associated problems.** This covers Singapore's pre-independence period, including its ill-fated merger with Malaya. There was little substantive change in the hawking policy landscape vis-à-vis Phase 1, except for a deeper understanding as to the motivations behind hawking and a greater impetus for hawker reform in Phase 3.

- **Phase 3 (1965 to present): Hawker reform through formalisation and sweeping enforcement.** Phase 3 saw the most significant developments within the nation and the hawking industry. This was during the post-colonial era, beginning when Lee Kuan Yew's People's Action Party (PAP) came to power and formed Singapore's independent government, introducing legislation and policies such as licensing and hawker centres that have remained until today.

In Phases 1 and 2, only hawking-specific (micro) policies were employed to control the sector, whereas in Phase 3, we see a combination of both micro- and macro-policies.

The second framework is that of the main instruments of control used by Singapore's administrations across all three phases. The first instrument is *policy*, which refers to legislation designed specifically for the control and improvement of hawking, particularly related to food hygiene and spatial restrictions. Policy is important as it sets the principles of regulating a practice and allows the government to deter and punish non-compliant behaviour.

The second instrument is that of *licensing and enforcement.* Licensing facilitates the bureaucratisation and rationalisation of hawkers as administrative subjects. This allows enforcers to identify, monitor, and if necessary, sanction them — a process that is essential for proper governance and the eventual formalisation of the hawking industry. Enforcers here refers to any agent of state authority, from the police to specialised health enforcement bodies.

The third instrument is that of *physical shelters,* such as hawker shelters and hawker centres, which allow the state to provide amenities such as washing and sanitation facilities and standardised hygiene equipment. Physical shelters agglomerate hawkers into one building, mitigating the issues of urban pollution and facilitating the efficient monitoring and enforcement of policies and rules. For this book, we refer to temporary short-term shelters as 'hawker shelters', most prevalent before 1965, and facilities typically built after independence to house hawkers permanently as 'hawker centres', existing in consideration with longer-term urban planning and other public utilities. Table 2.1 shows a compilation of the various phases, administrations and key archival documents.

Table 2.1.   Overview of the Key Phases, Reports and Instruments

Categories	Phase 1: Origins (1819–1942)	Phase 2: Growth (1942–1965)	Phase 3: Hawker Reform to Present (1965 onwards)
Administration	Colonial Administration (Straits Settlement Crown Colony)	Limited Self Governance (e.g., City Council, Singapore in Malaysia)	Independent Singapore (PAP)
Hawker Reports	1932 Report of the Committee Appointed to Investigate the Hawker Question in Singapore	Report of the Hawkers Inquiry Commission, 1950	Ministry of Environment / Hawkers Department Annual Reports, 1959–1974; Hawker Statistics 1974–1979
Instrument 1: Policy	Compulsory licensing and hawker shelters	Compulsory licensing and hawker shelters	Licensing, hawker-specific legislation, enforcement and hawker centres
Instrument 2: Licensing and Enforcement	Weak enforcement	Weak enforcement	Substantial enforcement by Hawkers Department
Instrument 3: Physical Shelters	Six temporary shelters constructed from 1922 to 1942	Temporary shelters in various areas with low uptake	Rapid build-up of hawker centres from 1960s to 1979. Hawkers must operate in hawker centres

Source: Ryan Kueh 2024, compiled from various sources such as the Straits Settlement Annual Report 1951; Report of the Hawkers Inquiry Commission 1950; Ministry of Environment/ Hawkers Department (HD) Annual Report 1971–1973; Ministry of Environment/Hawkers Department (HD) Statistics on Hawker Licences 1979; Ministry of Environment/Hawkers Department (HD) Statistics on Hawker Licences 1979.

As we will come to see, Singapore, in its decades-long administration of hawking, has repeatedly engaged with the three instruments of control, with the first two administrations' attempts being unsuccessful. Only the newly independent Singaporean government was successful in addressing the issues associated with hawking, managing to permanently reduce hawker population density whilst retaining hawking's socioeconomic and cultural functions. What this suggests is that micro-policies specifically targeted at hawking are insufficient and can only symptomatically treat the 'hawker problem'. The root causes of the problem, poverty and a lack of economic opportunity, must be addressed for there to be a permanent improvement in hawker population density. In this regard, we will come to see how the PAP government was successful in effecting this, employing both micro- and macro-policies simultaneously during Singapore's post-independence years.

Conclusion

Hawking as a general phenomenon is typically an informal and highly mobile trade. It is dually driven by exogenous circumstances, such as local demand for affordable, easily available cooked food, and entrepreneurial responses to a lack of alternative economic opportunities and social support. Given its informality, hawking often gives rise to disruptions to public order, public health concerns and spatial disorder. Thereafter, hawking population density may serve as a barometer of a nation's economic well-being, where there exists a general relationship between poor macroeconomic conditions and a higher prevalence of hawking. Hawker policy is typically formulated via two approaches: First, by improving the overall economic conditions of the country; second, by developing hawker-specific policies to regulate the proper development of the sector. Finally, we discussed the book's methodology, which utilises various approaches to uncover the history of Singapore's hawking phenomenon. Assisting us are two frameworks: First, a temporal one, splitting Singapore's hawking development into three phases; and the second, an administrative one, understanding hawker control through the instruments of policy, licensing and enforcement and physical shelters.

Chapter 3
Origins of Hawking in Singapore (Ninth to 14ᵗʰ Century)

{iconography: cutlery symbol}

The conventional narrative of hawking history in Singapore runs as follows: The sector emerged in the early 1800s, pioneered by enterprising migrants and locals seeking to make a living in the colonial port city. This narrative is commonly espoused by Singapore's heritage and tourism boards,[1] largely influenced by local academic Lily Kong's 2007 work, *Singapore Hawker Centres: People, Places, Food*.[2] However, in light of the growing conversation around nationhood and decolonisation within Singapore, it is perhaps timely to reconsider the association of hawking's origins with British colonialism. Archaeological evidence suggests that the older empires which governed the island before its colonisation ('ancient Singapore') were already regional trading hubs, possibly providing an environment conducive to hawking.

This chapter thus aims to challenge the prevailing narrative of hawking history, seeking to answer two questions: Did hawking exist even before colonial times? Can we go back further, and if so, how much? To do this, we study two approximate periods of Singapore's history: around the 14ᵗʰ century, as part of the Kingdom of Singapura; and around the ninth century as part of the Srivijaya Empire. Through analysis of literary and archaeological evidence, we seek to understand whether ancient Singapore fostered the conditions necessary for hawking even before the colonial era. To accomplish this, we will begin by examining the essential conditions for hawking, before delving into a discussion of the specific time periods.

Preconditions for Hawking

Hawking would have likely existed insofar as three main preconditions were met. These are:

1. Transient travellers and merchants looking to trade.

2. A local market that facilitates trade. This gives local artisans a platform to peddle goods and services to locals and foreigners.

3. The existence of currency to facilitate transactions.

The presence of these preconditions in ancient Singapore opens up the possibility of hawking existing since before colonial times. Hawking would have been encouraged by the circulation of transient visitors within the empires, as ports which engaged in regional trade would have routinely hosted transient visitors or merchants. A market within the port would have facilitated such interactions, further encouraging the conditions for hawkers to thrive. Transient visitors would not have the means to cook their own food, and thus would likely have needed to purchase cooked food. Locals would usually fill this service gap, selling food, drinks or other products out of inns, street carts or markets to travellers.

Thus, what we are looking for is evidence of whether ancient Singapore was already a regional trading hub that routinely hosted transient immigrants. Put another way, to ascertain the existence of hawkers in ancient Singapore, we must investigate whether their presence would have been supported by the settlement's economic conditions.

Pre-14ᵗʰ Century Singapore

The most probable period for the existence of hawking in ancient Singapore dates to somewhere around the 14ᵗʰ century, during the time of the Kingdom of Singapura (1299–1398). Known then as Temasik, the city was one of the primary trading and shipping sites along the Straits of Malacca.[3] Its growth began between 1000 to 1300, when cities along the Malaccan Straits underwent fundamental changes.[4] Asian maritime trade experienced rapid growth due to a shift in China's policy towards outward trade, encouraging merchants to venture abroad and trade along the maritime route known as the *Silk Road of the Sea*.[5] Southeast Asian ports like Malacca, Sumatra and Temasik played significant roles in facilitating trade within the region. These ports were popular destinations for Chinese merchants to trade with Arab merchants from the West.

Given China's strict entry controls for foreign visitors, many Arab visitors and merchants visited Sumatra and other nearby ports, with Sumatran embassies often acting as intermediaries between Chinese and Muslim traders.[6] These embassies would bring Arab products to China as tribute. One record mentions how, in 1018, one embassy brought 81,680 units of frankincense and other items from Arab lands, alongside Indonesian products such as pepper, nutmeg, sandalwood and cloves. Another mentions Sumatran embassies bringing 11 glass vessels (presumably from Arabia or the Persian Gulf) containing sugar, dates and gardenia flowers. While this is a Sumatran example, it is likely that other ports within the region played similar functions. Southeast Asian ports had deep connections with the regional economy, linked to a vast network of markets that connected regions such as Java, Sri Lanka, China and the Middle East. Often, merchants would stop by these ports of call to engage in trade, bringing foreign goods and wares, but more importantly, a stream of short-term foreign travellers to these cities.

By the early 14ᵗʰ century, Temasik was estimated to have around 10,000 residents, making it a medium-sized port for its time.[7] The city was intertwined with the regional economy,

> *"…firmly attached to a network of suppliers and markets stretching as far as Java, Sri Lanka, and China. Participants in this network would have needed a wide range of information about techniques of production, prices, market conditions, and sources of materials."*[8]

Temasik both serviced and competed with other prominent shipping and trading ports in the region, such as Malacca, Johor, Bintan, Jambi,

Palembang and Banten. Like other cosmopolitan ports in the Nusantara, Temasik too, was an important intermediary for Chinese and Western merchants to stop by and trade with one another within the city. These factors suggest that there was a relatively large and routine inflow of transient and permanent foreigners into Temasik. Two main pieces of evidence support this idea: historical accounts and archaeological findings.

Historical Accounts

In Derek Heng's 2002 article on Banzu (班卒, Fort Canning Hill), a Chinese settlement located north of the Singapore River, Heng analyses accounts from the *Daoyi Zhilue* by Wang Dayuan and the *Sejarah Melayu* (Malay Annals), both of which highlight Temasik's vitality as a trading port.[9] The *Sejarah Melayu* mentions the presence of a market within the settlement which was central to the import and export of goods. Wang Dayuan further mentions a locally-produced alcoholic spirit called *ming-jia*, made from fermented rice, which was likely sold in the same market. This is particularly interesting as Temasik's terroir does not support growing grain, which meant that the rice used to make this spirit was likely grown elsewhere and imported. The accounts also mention other commonly traded items such as sea slugs and hornbill casques, products which were harvested and traded regionally within the Malay Peninsula and Riau Archipelago. Wang writes this of the Banzu Settlement[10]:

> *"This locality is the hill back of Lung-ya mên, it is like a coil cut off [at the top], it rises to a hollow-topped summit enclosed in a series of [rising] slopes; as a consequence, the people live all around it. The soil is poor and grain rather scarce. The climate is not regular, for it rains a great deal in summer when it is rather cool. The people are straightforward. They wear their hair short with a turban of gold brocaded satin, and a red oiled cloth wound around the body. They boil sea-water to make salt, and ferment rice to make a kind of spirits [sic] called ming-kia*

(明家). They have a ruler. The native products include cranes' crests of superior quality, middling quality lakawood, and cotton. The goods used in trading are green cotton stuff (录布), pieces of iron, native cotton prints, dark red gold (紫金) porcelain-ware, iron pots, and such like things…"[11]

Wang also wrote a separate assessment of Longyamen (龙牙门, Keppel Strait), where he observed a significant difference compared to the Banzu Settlement. Within Longyamen, he recorded the presence of Chinese settlers residing alongside the Orang Laut community,[12] where the absence of ethnic segregation was uncommon for Malay trading-port settlements. Wang mentioned that:

"The soil is poor and paddy fields few…Men and women live mixed up among the Chinese… The natural products of the country are coarse laka-wood and tin (斗錫). The goods used [by the Chinese] in trading here are red gold, blue satin, cotton prints, Ch'u-chou-fa porcelain, iron caldrons, and such like things. Neither fine products nor rare objects come from here."[13]

The settlement observed in Longyamen is particularly intriguing: It suggests that Temasik was sufficiently well-known in the region, capable of enticing early Chinese immigrants to settle in overseas lands. During these resettlements, it was likely that Chinese settlers brought over their own homeware, with Chu-Chou porcelain (also known as southern celadon or Longquan-type celadon) found amongst these settlements, indicating its importation and use by the Chinese during their travels to the Malaccan Straits. The usage of Chu-Chou porcelain also suggests that the Chinese inhabitants were from regions surrounding Guangdong, as Chu-Chou porcelain was initially made in Longquan (龙泉 or 龍泉).[14]

The presence of Chu-Chou porcelain supports the notion of interregional trade and migration during the Southern Song Period (1127–1279).[15] Chinese porcelain was in demand due to its diverse colours, popular amongst locals, clergy and temples. Green and white wares were favoured in Java, green porcelain in Borneo and white wares in the Eastern Indonesian archipelago. By the 13th century, Chinese porcelain was routinely exported to various regions, including Southeast Asia (north Vietnam, Cambodia, San Foqi and the northern Malay peninsula), South Asia and even as far as Zanzibar. In sum, historical accounts support the notion of trading activity and immigration within Temasik, with a seemingly routine flow of the import and export of local goods through its market.

Archaeological Findings

Broader archaeological excavations support Temasik's consistent engagement with China, regional empires and the Middle East. Numerous fragments of green-glazed wares with a double fish motif have been uncovered within the Longyamen area, and a high concentration of melted glass fragments, resin and shards of mercury jars were also found in Banzu. Other artefacts include gold ornaments, such as gold armlets, a plaque of *repoussé* work with a Javanese Kala head, and gold jewellery like rings and ornaments containing inferior jewels, reminiscent of 14th century Majapahit craftsmanship.[16] Findings of such artefacts are in consilience with the political happenings of that era, when the Javanese from Majapahit captured Singapore from the Srivijaya Empire. British Orientalist Richard Windstedt opined that it is "quite certain that these ornaments belong to that era,"[17] with Heng further supporting that these crafts were likely made by foreign craftsmen employed by the settlement's ruler.[18]

A second notable archaeological finding is the Houzhu shipwreck, excavated near the city of Quanzhou in 1974, which offers valuable insights into the preferences of Chinese merchants vis-à-vis Southeast Asian goods and sheds light on historical maritime trade in the region.[19] The ship is estimated to have had a crew of 50 sailors back in its day, carrying cargo primarily originating from Southeast Asia. The largest categories of preserved items comprised organic materials (spices, pepper), medicinal substances (betel nuts, frankincense, ambergris), aromatic wood (laka, sandalwood, gharu) and tortoise shells. Only a few Chinese objects (porcelain, pottery) were found on board, alongside over 2,000 cowries, which may have been used as currency for trade in Southeast Asia. This is interesting as the Chinese did not use cowries as currency domestically, suggesting that there was a separate currency within the region used specifically for trade with the Malayan empires.

Archaeological findings also suggest that Temasik maintained interactions with regional partners such as Java and Thailand.[20] Excavations in Singapore have yielded shards of pottery from East Java, discovered at a find site within the present-day Old Parliament House, also known as The Arts House. These fragments resemble the high-quality red earthenware commonly found in places like Trowulan and other Javanese sites. Conversely, Temasik-made earthenware has been identified in Java, including shreds of intentionally chipped pottery known as *gacuk* found in Majapahit's capital. Aside from Javanese items, a variety of pottery types from the Siam Empire have been found in Singapore. These include fine paste ware and glazed pottery, which have also been found across many regions in Southeast Asia, including the Philippines, South Thailand and Kedah.

A last, noteworthy discovery involves the unearthing of foreign coins in Singapore. Archaeologists uncovered two Sri Lankan coins within Singapore, with one found in the 1995 Parliament House Complex excavation alongside a large quantity of Chinese coins. The site of the compound previously served as a commercial and industrial area in 14ᵗʰ century Temasik, suggesting a presence of copperworking activities that likely involved the use of Chinese coins for daily transactions.[21] Archaeologist John Miksic interprets these findings as evidence of significant economic and political interactions between the Straits of Malacca and its regional partners, "demonstrat[ing] that the local economy was sufficiently sophisticated that more than one type of currency [was] in circulation."[22] This reinforces the notion that Temasik served as a bustling port with trade connections to various regions. Although we cannot ascertain the details of transactions within these markets, such findings support the notion that trade was facilitated through some form of currency, supporting the idea that Temasik had a complex role in the regional economy with currencies used for commerce within local markets.

Hawking in 14th Century Temasik

It was likely that hawking existed around and during 14th century Singapore. Temasik's integration into the regional economy, coupled with its dependency on foreign trade, supports the conditions necessary for the existence of hawkers. To restate, the conditions are:

1. Transient travellers and merchants looking to trade.

2. A local market that facilitates trade. This gives local artisans a platform to peddle goods and services to locals and foreigners.

3. The existence of some form of currency to facilitate transactions.

Accounts of Temasik align with these three conditions. Archaeological findings suggest that Temasik thrived as a trading hub, frequently hosting visits from regional, Middle Eastern and Chinese merchants, and actively engaging in the exchange of foreign and locally produced goods. Secondly, historical records affirm the presence of a marketplace. Accounts from the *Sejarah Melayu* and Wang Dayuan highlight the existence of a marketplace in the heart of Temasik, where foreign merchants could trade with the local population. Finally, foreign currencies such as cowries, Sri Lankan coins and Chinese coins were found across or nearby Temasik, both suggesting that currency-based transactions rather than barter arrangements were carried out. Moreover, trade would also have been essential for the city port's sustenance. As described by historical accounts, the populous city, lacking a substantial resource hinterland, would have needed to rely heavily on foreign trade for its survival. Early explorers such as Wang Dayuan and Tomé Pires emphasised Temasik's lack of autarkic capabilities,[23] with findings of ceramics, porcelain, religious architecture and sculptures in trading-port settlements across the broader Malayan region supporting the concept of a thriving regional trade network and patterns of immigration. Piecing these fragments of information together, there is strong evidence supporting the existence of hawking within or around 14th century Singapore.

Srivijaya Singapore and the Tang Shipwreck

Having explored the potential existence of hawkers around the 14th century, we challenge ourselves to examine whether hawkers existed even earlier in Singapore's history. Here, we broaden our inquiry to around the ninth century, seeking older evidence of conditions supporting hawking in Singapore. Assisting us in this endeavour is the Tang Shipwreck, or Belitung Shipwreck, an archaeological marvel that hints towards the presence of global maritime trade as early as the ninth century. Discovered by Indonesian fishermen 610 kilometres off Singapore's coast in 1998, the Tang Shipwreck houses valuable insights that enhance our understanding of the region's trading significance. It alludes to the existence of an alternative maritime trade route — the Maritime Silk Road — during the ninth century, a distinct route from the overland Silk Road between China and the Middle East.[24] This maritime route positioned Southeast Asia as a pivotal trading waypoint for both Chinese and Middle Eastern merchants. The question we must then answer is whether Singapore was a key port within this pivotal waypoint during this period.

The contents onboard the Tang Shipwreck suggest that the ship was carrying Chinese goods to the Middle East. An astounding 96% of the retrieved cargo is comprised of approximately 60,000 units of Changsha ceramics, with the ceramics on board distinctive from that of other wrecks. Dates imprinted on the bowls date them to between 826 and 850.[25] This variety of ceramic was extensively manufactured for export during the Tang Dynasty (618–907) and has surfaced not only in Southeast Asia but also in regions spanning modern-day Korea, Japan, India, the Middle East and Africa. The cargo of the Tang Shipwreck suggests that the ship may have been delivering a bulk order of Changsha ceramics from Guangzhou or Yangzhou in China to the Abbasid Caliphate (modern-day Iran and Iraq).[26] Aside from Changsha ceramics, objects of Southeast Asian provenance — grindstone and a roller, aromatic resin, a scales bar, scales weights and a piloncito gold coin — were also found, supporting the idea that the Tang ship visited other Southeast Asian ports during its journey.[27] However, the ship's final resting place in Belitung, Indonesia does not lie along the most direct course between China and the Middle East. This complicates the suggestion that the Abbasid Caliphate was its potential destination, as most common shipping routes to the Middle East would go through Singapore and the Straits of Malacca. In the case of the Tang Shipwreck, the ship seemed to have intentionally made a detour to the Java Sea, presumably for trade.

Academics have described the shipwreck as a puzzle given its unique characteristics — "Chinese cargo on an Arab ship, sunken in Southeast Asia."[28] The ship's construction technique indicates that the vessel was not of Chinese origin but from somewhere in the Persian Gulf or the Western Indian Ocean.[29] Such a multicultural phenomenon was not common during this era. One hypothesis is that ports along the maritime trade route were already bustling cosmopolitan trading hubs since the seventh century.[30] Stephen Murphy points to the cosmopolitanism of coastal cities then, such as Guangzhou and Yangzhou, which were known to contain diverse ethnic communities such as Arabs, Malays, Chams and Indians, and featured multiple religions such as Islam, Christianity, Judaism, Hinduism and Buddhism. This Tang ship was perhaps a microcosm of such cosmopolitanism, with the uncovered artefacts suggesting a diverse crew comprising sailors from the Middle East, East Asia and Southeast Asia.

Literary records and archaeological evidence further support the probability of regional Southeast Asian hubs during this period.[31] One such nexus was the Bujang Valley in Kedah, northern Malaysia. Positioned at the heart of maritime trade within the Thai–Malay peninsula, the Bujang Valley was a strategic locale where goods could be traded and exchanged, connecting trans-peninsular routes to entrepôts along the Gulf of Thailand. Records mentioning the location of the valley date back to the seventh century Sui Court, with its location also mentioned in ninth century Arabic texts that refer to the Bujang Valley as Kalah and Kataha. Both Middle Eastern and Chinese artefacts have been found within the valley, with discoveries such as Chinese mirrors, Tang ceramics, Arab glass and turquoise Persian earthenware unearthed. Another significant trading port was Barus in northwest Sumatra, which has produced the largest amount of Near Eastern artefacts within the region. Gold, silver jewellery, coins, Buddhist statues and ancient inscriptions of Tamil and Javanese have been found there. Elsewhere, Chinese artefacts have surfaced in Southern Vietnam (Con Dau Island and Tra Kieu) and the Philippines (Butuan and Mindanao).[32]

Closer to Singapore, salient finds have also been reported from Palembang, where several shards of Middle Eastern ceramic and glass dating back between the late 11ᵗʰ century to the mid-13ᵗʰ century have been found in Kota Cina, northeast Sumatra. Palembang, the capital of the Srivijaya Empire, was one of the other prominent pit stops along the maritime trade route. Srivijaya's maritime influence extended throughout the region, with Murphy suggesting that the Tang ship was perhaps en route to or departing from Palembang.[33] Spices found in Srivijaya were likely the goods that merchants were seeking due to their high profitability and low weight, potentially explaining the ship's diversion from its usual course.

None of these findings, however, hinted towards the land of Singapore itself being one of such ports. Archaeological remnants dating to the ninth century or earlier have not been found within Singapore yet, suggesting that Singapore may not have supported the conditions for hawking then. One possible reason for ninth century Singapore's lack of trading prowess was due to Palembang's superiority over Singapore. Given that both cities were part of the Srivijaya Empire then, Palembang would have been a priority node for the Srivijaya Empire to consolidate goods and trade outwardly. Altogether, the presence of the Tang Shipwreck and onshore findings hint towards the existence of regular interregional trade within Southeast Asia, supporting the conditions for hawking within prominent regional ports such as Palembang and the Bujang Valley. However, the same cannot be confirmed for Singapore, where there is a lack of evidence supporting the notion that the island was one of such maritime gateways around the ninth century. Ultimately, our understanding of this period remains limited, a situation that could potentially change if more literary or archaeological evidence is discovered and which hints towards Singapore being a trading hub within the region.

Conclusion

Archaeological and historical evidence indicate that hawking existed around 14th century Singapore. Within Temasik, archaeological evidence underscores Singapore's role as a regional mercantile hub, serving as a significant port of call within the region. This position facilitated trade interactions for regional, Chinese and Middle Eastern traders. Given the influx of external visitors, a market for the trade of locally crafted items and imported goods, and the presence of currencies for trade, Singapore around the 14th century fulfilled the three preconditions for hawking to exist. However, the same cannot be confidently said for the period around ninth century Singapore. Although maritime routes then were already heavily operated by traders, Singapore was likely not one of their ports of call and was unlikely to support the three preconditions for hawking to exist. What we *can* potentially conclude, however, is that regional trading ports were ethnically and racially diverse, which meant that visitors from surrounding areas were abundant. Hawking was more likely to have occurred in other regional ports such as Palembang, Surabaya, Guangzhou or Yangzhou.

As such, the existence of hawkers dates back hundreds of years before the establishment of the first colonial outpost in the country, reinforcing the notion that essential aspects of Singapore's contemporary identity need not necessarily originate from the British's first landing in Singapore. Tapping into this narrative provides us insights into the origins of hawking as a trade, centuries before Singapore's colonisation. These insights play a pivotal role in Singapore's decolonisation discourse, enabling a deeper engagement with the nation's history independent of colonial narratives.

Chapter 4
Phase 1: Colonial Singapore (1819 to 1942)

🍴

"There is probably no city in the world with such a motley crowd of itinerant vendors of wares, fruits, cakes, vegetables. There are Malays, generally with fruit, Chinamen with a mixture of all sorts, and Klings with cakes and different kinds of nuts. Malays and Chinamen always use the shoulder-stick, having equally-balanced loads suspended at either end; the Klings, on the contrary, carry their wares on the head on trays."[1]

Some of our earliest perspectives on hawkers can be attributed to John Cameron, then-owner and editor of national broadsheet *The Straits Times*. The above description by Cameron is one of the earliest written accounts in English of hawkers in Singapore, portraying a vibrant hawking landscape with a medley of vendors from different ethnicities and cultures in 1865. This is the oft-referenced starting point for hawking in Singapore, one that aligns itself with Singapore's colonial conception of nationhood. Despite disrupting this narrative in Chapter 3, there remains great historical utility in delving into hawking during this period given the British's extensive bookkeeping of developments in Singapore, which allows us to trace changes in hawking within the colony. As this chapter will reveal, Cameron's seemingly idyllic hawking scene would eventually evolve into a complex phenomenon with substantial social, public health and political implications. This chapter seeks to establish a foundational understanding of the hawking landscape during the early colonial period encompassing the years 1819–1942. We will delve into the factors contributing to the surge of hawking during the period and analyse the sociological consequences that accompanied said surge.

Colonial Singapore

Under the colonial administration, Singapore was a burgeoning entrepôt trading centre in the middle of Southeast Asia.[2] During the 19th century, the region witnessed extensive maritime engagement propelled by jostling Portuguese, Dutch and English trading companies, ultimately accounting for nearly 25% of the British East India Company's overall volume of trade in the 1820s. Singapore regularly featured vessels from the Malay peninsula, Celebes, eastern Java, the Gulf of Siam and Indo-China, enmeshed in the multitude of regional maritime activity that connected the Arab lands and India to the West and China to the east. By the end of the late 19th century, Singapore had become a well-established port. It not only imported goods from Siam, Burma and Indochina for the Malayan and Dutch East Indies, but also exported its own raw materials such as tin, rubber and petroleum.

As Singapore's trade volume increased, so did its population. To fuel the continued expansion of trade activity, the port city adopted an open immigration policy that enabled easy movement of traders and workers. This quickly changed the ethnic makeup of the city-port from being predominantly Malay to one that increasingly accommodated Chinese and Indians. When the British first arrived in 1819, the population was described in the following terms:

> *"...about 150 fishermen and pirates, living in a few miserable huts; about thirty were Chinese, the remainder Malays... [The population] rapidly increased in less than one year to nearly 5000, principally Chinese; and in November 1822, we are informed by Sir S. Raffles that the population of the town of Singapore had amounted to least 10,000 inhabitants."*[3]

Chinese migration to Singapore began in the early 19th century, mainly from the southern provinces of Guangdong (广东) and Fujian (福建). Having been displaced by pressures such as the Taiping Rebellion and long-term economic depression, these coastal dwellers were attracted by the prospect of economic opportunity and upward mobility in the Malaccan Straits. The establishment of the British colony in Singapore spurred large inflows of new migration from China to Singapore, motivated by these overseas provinces' early contact with British traders.[4] In the 1826 census of the city, colonial authorities already recorded more Chinese than Malays (excluding the Bugis and Javanese),[5] with the rise in Chinese and Indian immigrants shifting the demographic proportions in Singapore. By the turn of the 20th century, the Chinese constituted around 72% of the population, with this proportion generally remaining till today.[6]

For reference, in the 1890s, only about 10% of Chinese in Singapore were locally born. Immigrants were mostly males aged 15 to 59 who had travelled overseas without family in hopes of finding employment. Most of these men — who constituted most of the working population — came alone and were jobless and indebted upon arrival. By the early 1900s, Southeast Asia accounted for around 70% of Chinese emigrants across the world, with Singapore emerging as the world's second largest Chinese community by proportion, behind only China itself.[7]

Like the Chinese, the prospect of a new British colony attracted Indian immigration into Singapore, driven by male coolies seeking alternative economic opportunities. At one point, Indians were the second largest community in Singapore, totalling 13,000 in the 1860s, before falling behind the Chinese and Malays in the early 1900s.[8] The bulk of Indian immigrants consisted of young males, mostly traders or labourers from South India.[9] Other immigrants were brought over by the British administration to fill the positions of clerks (Sri Lankan Tamils, Malayalees), merchants (Sindhis, Gujaratis, Tamil Muslims), tradesmen and soldiers. A final group of immigrants included penal immigrants, Indian convicts who served their sentences by carrying out manual labour in Singapore. This 'forced migration' followed the Anglo-Dutch Treaty of 1824, where the British traded Bencoolen (present-day

Bengkulu City in Indonesia) for the Dutch colony of Malacca, resulting in the closing of a British penal colony. Convict labour was used to build infrastructure in Singapore, such as Saint Andrew's Cathedral (1862) and the Istana (1869).[10] Upon completing their sentences, individuals had the choice of staying within the port city or returning to India.

Hawkers in Colonial Singapore

The large influx of overseas immigrants contributed to a rise in both demand for hawking as a service and the supply of hawker labour. As the number of immigrants increased, so did structural and frictional unemployment, driven by a natural disequilibrium in economic growth and economic opportunity which motivated individuals to explore alternative avenues of employment during periods of transition. Hawking flourished in colonial Singapore for two main reasons.

First, on the supply side, hawking emerged as a relatively attractive trade: a flexible job characterised by low barriers to entry, demanding minimal skills and capital investment whilst yielding respectable earnings.[11] Starting a hawking enterprise was relatively straightforward. In its simplest form, one only required common ingredients and a vehicle to transport (such as a basket or a pushcart) and sell the finished dishes. The ease of starting a hawking business attracted many in need of alternative employment. For example, one could sell homemade food whilst concurrently exploring alternative employment prospects. As a vocation, hawking also served the authorities' interests by providing work for the unemployed, contributing to the general productivity of the masses. Second, hawkers provided affordable and convenient food for labourers in the city. These labourers, mostly male immigrants without families, had neither the time, social support structures (e.g., family) nor space to encourage them to cook for themselves. Cooked food hawkers filled this service gap by providing these workers with cheap and convenient meals.

Two main types of hawkers existed in Singapore.[12] The first category was *basket hawkers*, who constituted the dominant group of cooked food hawkers. These mobile and itinerant hawkers offered simple fare (e.g., rice cakes, *iddipyam*, and fried *bee hoon*) directly from baskets slung over their shoulders. The second category comprised *pushcart hawkers*, distinguished by their stationary presence or established routes. Pushcarts allowed hawkers to offer more substantial fare, including hot dishes such as *char kway teow* and fishball noodles, and even soup-based dishes such as *mee rebus* and *mee siam*. Strategically locating themselves within crowded areas to attract more business, hawkers predominantly established their locations in the city centre and around the docks, providing mid-day labourers with breakfast and lunch options. (Dinner was not as popular as the workers would have ended their shifts and returned to their homes, leading to a smaller customer base.) As the port of Singapore grew, so did the importance of hawkers, who played a crucial role in nourishing the workforce driving Singapore's evolving landscape and established themselves as a vital ancillary of the expanding economy.

Distribution of Hawkers

Hawkers would have been distributed in two main patterns. The first key pattern hawkers followed was agglomerating within the business district, servicing the working crowd. As we will see later, this would come to be the locus of the administration's problems. Ethnic or dialect districts would have been the second key areas where hawkers congregated, as these core residential areas were likely the locations with the next-highest footfall; it might also have been convenient for the hawkers themselves if they lived nearby.

The distribution of coffeeshops (*kopitiams* in local vernacular), an organised and formal contemporary of the hawkers, supports this proposed spatial distribution pattern. They were privately owned stalls, run by vendors who had often rented a shophouse or shopfront to sell food and drinks. Coffeeshops had a distinct ethnic dimension which broadly aligned with immigrants' residential enclaves.[13] During this period, most members of an ethnic group stayed with others of the same ethnicity. The city was ethnically clustered by district, with distinct neighbourhoods such as Chinatown for the Chinese, Little India for the Indians and Kampong Glam for the Muslims. Within the Chinese population, this clustering was further segmented into dialect groups,[14] with major dialect groups such as the Hokkiens, Teochews and Cantonese settling themselves south of the Singapore River (the so-called South Bank), whilst smaller dialect groups such as the Hainanese, Foochow and Henghuas established themselves on the north of the Singapore River.

Two markets elucidate this point. The first is the Ellenborough Market (see Figure 4.1), the second-oldest market after Telok Ayer Market. Erected in 1845 on the South Bank, it was alternatively referred to as 'Teochew Market' or 'Pasar Bahru' (New Market), renowned for its Teochew food offerings and merchandise.[15] Ellenborough Market was primarily a wet market noted for its fresh fish and dried seafood products, selling ingredients commonly used in Teochew dishes and featuring hawker stalls specialising in Teochew food. The second example is the former Tekka Market (see Figure 4.2), also known as 'Kandang Kerbau Market' in Malay or 'Mattu Kampong Pasar', located in Little India.[16] Tekka Market, which was constructed in 1915 and mainly serviced the Indian and Indian-Muslim population, was renowned for its wide variety of meat, seafood and vegetables. Given their ability to attract crowds, it is likely that these markets were hotspots for itinerant hawkers (see Figure 4.3). It is worth noting that these markets are different from the cooked food specific hawker shelters that will be discussed later in this text, with wet markets intended for the sale of all types of produce and goods.

Figure 4.1.   Ellenborough Market, Singapore (1910)

Source: Courtesy of National Archives of Singapore.

Figure 4.2.   Mutton Stalls along Serangoon Road (1982)

Source: Courtesy of National Archives of Singapore.

Figure 4.3.   A Group of Chinese Hawkers, Singapore (1915; Phase 1 of the development of Singapore's hawking sector)

Source: Courtesy of National Archives of Singapore.

Rise of the 'Hawker Problem'

Waves of migration caused Singapore's population to grow exponentially, resulting in a rise in hawker numbers and a build-up in urban density that exacerbated hawking-related issues. The population jumped eighteen-fold in less than a century, going from 16,634 in 1830 to 303,321 in 1901, before roughly doubling to 557,745 in 1931.[17] As the number of hawkers increased, so did the absolute number of people in structural and frictional unemployment, increasing the propensity for hawking. Population growth also meant more mouths to feed, increasing the demand for hawking services.

In 1913, demand for hawking strengthened further after the licensing of coffeeshops was transferred from the police to the municipal health authorities.[18] Compared to the police, the municipal health authorities held coffeeshops to higher standards of hygiene and scrutiny, with the authorities issuing fewer licences as time went by. As a result, the number of coffeeshops fell by around 66%, from 1,520 in 1914 to 515 in 1922, heavily reducing the availability of affordable food within the city. This, coupled with the city's growing population, ultimately amplified the demand for cooked food hawkers.

The growing hawker population presented multiple challenges for the municipal authorities. In 1913, Dr. W.R.C Middleton, a municipal health officer, described these hawker-related challenges as "evils", specifically referring to the "obstruction of streets and five-foot ways, the selling of food in a manner rendering it liable to contamination, and the fouling of streets and five-foot ways".[19] In essence, hawking created two key issues for authorities: (1) public health issues and (2) urban pollution issues.

First, hawkers presented risks to public health, being linked to the spread of diseases such as cholera and typhoid.[20] As the *1932 Report by the Committee Appointed to Investigate the Hawker Question in Singapore* stated:

> *"The hawkers of cooked food, and of certain other edible articles such as ice-cream and ice-drinks, are objected to on health grounds, as the conditions both of preparation and distribution render the food liable to be contaminated. What the effect of this from a health point of view is, it has not been possible to ascertain, but the use in succession by the customers, of inadequately washed utensils must be a fruitful source of infection, as must be also surroundings in which the food is cooked in many cases."*[21]

Most hawkers engaged in unsanitary food and drink preparation practices. For example, they would use contaminated water sources to prepare food and drinks and wash utensils, increasing the risk of foodborne diseases. Often, they disposed of waste by pouring it into drains, clogging drainage systems and choking proper sanitary channels, encouraging the spread of rodents and public health diseases.

Records from the Municipal Health Office in 1895 and the Sanitation Commission in 1907 reported hawkers operating close to drainage systems and amongst vermin,[22] a hazardous combination further exacerbated by low public inoculation against common diseases.

Second, hawkers posed challenges to urban planning. Large numbers of itinerant hawkers would cluster in high-traffic areas in unpredictable patterns, causing congestion for motor vehicles and pedestrians.[23] According to the 1932 Report, traffic congestion caused by hawkers primarily affected three main areas:

1. The Central Business District: Office spaces and warehouses near Raffles Square and Collyer Quay.

2. Congested downtown areas: Cantonment Road, Outram Road, Kim Seng Road, the Singapore River, Kampong Martin, Mohamed Sultan Road, Tank Road, Orchard Road to Railway Bridge to Newton Station.

3. Suburbs: Bukit Timah Road, Race Course Road, Lavender Street and along Kallang Road to Sir Arthur's Bridge.

Office areas bore the brunt of congestion and hygiene concerns, as hawkers would congregate there during mid-day to supply lunch to clerks, messengers and coolies. Additionally, given their general uncooperativeness and the scale of hawking within the area, efforts by the Town Cleansing Department to ameliorate the situation had limited effect. Hawkers would set up shop on varying days and times and sometimes in different locations, making it hard for municipal officers to issue them with licences, let alone enforce any form of regulation. Even then, attempts at enforcement would often result in a cat-and-mouse situation, with illegal hawkers dispersing upon spotting the authorities before setting up shop again once they had left. Coupled with a lack of comprehensive hawker regulation and low rates of education amongst hawkers, these issues persisted throughout the late 19th and early 20th centuries.[24]

Attempts at Addressing the Hawker Problem: Legislation and Shelters

To address these growing problems, the colonial authorities turned to two main instruments: legislation and hawker shelters. Legislation focused on controlling the supply of hawkers and regulating the conduct of hawking, whilst shelters were used to gather hawkers into centralised buildings in hopes of facilitating enforcement and monitoring.

With regard to legislation, the colonial authorities were the first to introduce mandatory licensing of itinerant hawkers, enacted through hawker-specific laws. Whilst the Chinese Protectorate had previously introduced hawker registration in 1903,[25] this only applied to Chinese hawkers, and oversight efforts were unsupported by municipal authorities who were unwilling to allocate resources for enforcement.[26] The responsibility for hawker oversight was officially transferred from the Chinese Protectorate to British Municipal Commissioners in 1907, who proposed and passed the first by-laws aimed at registering and regulating night hawkers on public streets.[27] These were largely ineffective, as the by-laws only applied to night hawkers — who made up but a fraction of the overall population, as most hawkers operated in the morning and mid-day to service the working crowd — with the laws eventually extending to both day and night hawkers 12 years later, in 1919.[28] Despite the new laws, hawkers were not compliant, with the Municipal Health Office still routinely reporting issues of food contamination, uncooperativeness amongst hawkers and traffic congestion within the city centre.[29]

Shelters, meanwhile, were a temporary way to ringfence the negative effects of hawking, providing the authorities with a way to better control hawkers whilst working on a longer-term policy (see Figure 4.4). Shelters served two main functions, the first being the regulation of hygiene standards. They offered standardised utilities and systems such as running water, the spatial separation of raw-food and cooked food hawkers and washing areas for hawkers to use, thereby increasing the overall base level of hygiene. Second, shelters facilitated spatial control by agglomerating hawkers in designated areas such as streets or buildings, moving itinerant hawkers away from congested areas. This introduced a degree of spatial discipline to prime areas and reduced congestion whilst simplifying enforcement for authorities. The first cooked food designated shelters were constructed at Finlayson Green in 1922, with five more shelters — People's Park Shelter, Balestier Road Shelter (1923), Carnie Road Shelter (1927), Telok Ayer Market (1928) and Queen Street Shelter (1929) — constructed by the end of World War II.[30]

Figure 4.4.   Fixed Pitch Stalls at Old Kallang Airport Estate (1963; Phase 2 of the development of Singapore's hawking sector)

Source: Ministry of Information and the Arts Collection, courtesy of National Archives of Singapore.

Years Leading Up to 1932 and the 1932 Report

Early municipal leaders had been intent on eradicating hawkers. In 1924, the Municipal Health Officer proposed a plan to eradicate street hawkers in Singapore, citing concerns about sanitation, congestion and competition with licensed eating establishments.[31] A second unsuccessful attempt at eradicating hawkers came again in 1928, when municipal commissioners tried to limit the number of itinerant hawker licences to 6,000, with the Chief Police Officer of the opinion that all itinerant hawkers should be removed from the streets, and hawkers confined to only operating in markets.[32] These proposals, however, were often met with fierce opposition from both hawkers and locals alike, and the proposals were eventually abandoned shortly after.

By 1932, the 113th year of British colonial rule, various administrations had attempted to solve problems associated with hawking for almost a century to no avail. Singapore's port, economy and population continued to grow, as did the number of hawkers. Attempts to ameliorate hawking-related problems through legislation and cooked food shelters in the 1910s and 1920s were inadequate. To better investigate and address the persistent hawking problem, the British conducted an inquiry, ultimately producing the 1932 Report on the Committee Appointed to Investigate the Hawker Question in Singapore. The report was the first comprehensive study done on the so-called 'hawker problem' by the colonial administration. Interviews were conducted with key stakeholders, including then-Municipal Health Officer Dr. P.S. Hunter; Assistant Superintendent Mr. Edwin Tongue; Mr. Seow Poh Leng, a representative from the Straits Chinese British Association; Mr. Lee Kim Soo, a merchant on behalf of the Chinese Chamber of Commerce, and others, including members from the various Chinese clan associations.

The 1932 Report marked a notable divergence from previous approaches to the hawking phenomenon. Specifically, it marked the first time the

British formally recognised the essential role of hawkers within the growing city. To that end, the Committee extensively presented arguments supporting the indispensability of hawkers, particularly in a dedicated section titled the "Need for Hawkers".[33] Here, the Committee argued for the continued presence of hawkers in the city, given their provision of cheap and convenient food to labourers and residents alike, with the report noting that "hawkers of fresh foods of various kinds are a great convenience to the residents, more especially to the class that keeps no servants."[34] This consideration was further informed by the dwindling number of coffeeshops, which reduced the availability of affordable food. The situation was especially pronounced around the Collyer Quay-Raffles Place district — one of the most congested areas — as it serviced a substantial portion of the Asian and Eurasian staff employed by European firms and businesses.[35]

The 1932 Report marked an attitudinal shift towards actively working to retain hawkers within the city, albeit only in the short term. In the long term, the administration still retained the possibility of eradicating hawkers owing to the multiplicity of issues that they brought about. Hawking was now seen as an immediate socioeconomic necessity, and the Committee sought to find a middle ground between servicing the need for hawkers and addressing the challenges they posed. To tackle ongoing challenges, they first re-emphasised the need for licensing, identification and regulation of hawkers (see Figure 4.5). Second, they wanted to further engage in the relocation of hawkers into specific cooked food shelters that would be established in congested areas. Third, the Committee also urged their counterparts in the Municipal Health Authorities to streamline the requirements for coffeeshops to the minimum compatible level. This was in hopes of encouraging the development of more coffeeshops to alleviate the demand for affordable food. In addition to these mitigating measures, the Committee also sought to impose a strict cap on the total number of hawker licences. The intent was not to suppress hawking entirely,

Figure 4.5.   Licence Belonging to Sitigun Binti Haji Idris, an Itinerant Hawker

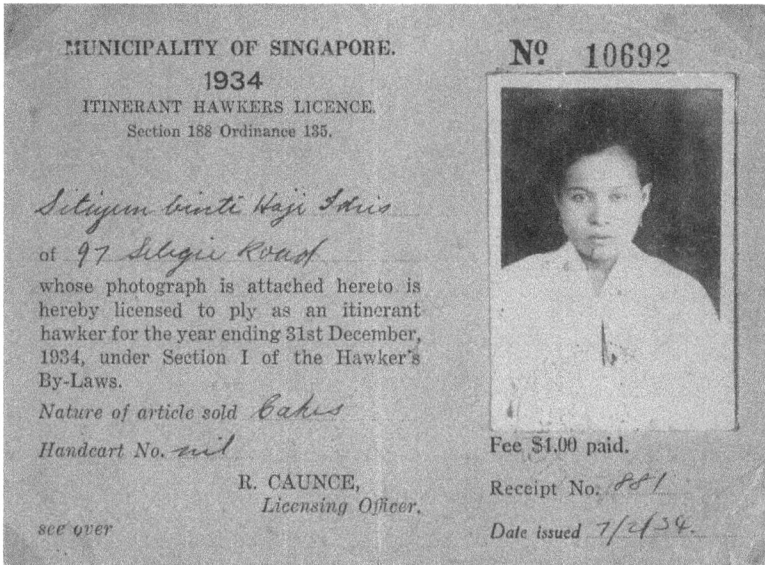

Source: Collection of the National Museum of Singapore, National Heritage Board. Gift of William Neo.

but to "reduce hawkers to a minimum and to confine hawking to particular localities where it could be controlled and monitored."[36] Their proposal entailed fixing the total number of hawker licences at 12,000, with a goal of reducing the number of licences by 10% per year until it reached "minimum necessity". It is unclear what this number was, although data cited in Chapter 2 would place this at about 1.5% to 2.5% of the population. As it stood in 1931, 12,000 hawkers would have meant a 2.17% hawker population density (based on a population of 562,866).[37]

Outcomes of the 1932 Report

Ultimately, these recommendations were largely rhetorical and had limited effect. Academic Brenda Yeoh has described them as "illusory", where the "growth of the hawker population appeared to have its own inexorable logic and every decrease in the number of licensed hawkers was counterbalanced by increases in the number of unlicensed hawkers."[38]

First, it made little economic sense for hawkers to pay licensing fees or shelter rents if it did not improve their profits. The cost for a licence for an itinerant hawker was one Straits Dollar a year and $48 for a stallholder.[39] Rent was $6 a month for stalls in shelters and $12 for three months for stalls on the roads. Such amounts were hefty for most cooked food hawkers, who only earned around 3–5 cents per serving of food,[40] with the potential reduction to their income even more significant if hawking was only a temporary job.

Second, the lack of compliance from hawkers and the weak enforcement capabilities of the colonial administration hindered the implementation of the 1932 Report's recommendations.[41] This affected the overall control of the hawker situation and its long-term development. The Committee was aware of this issue, where "[c]ertain provisions have been laid down for their control and for the limitation of their numbers, and there have been sporadic activity against them by the Police and Municipal authorities, but there has been nothing which could be dignified with the title of policy."[42] Gaps in the regulators' capabilities resulted in occasional scuffles between hawkers and authorities, leading to secondary problems such as bribery and the paying of protection fees to secret societies by hawkers to protect themselves from law enforcement. As the subsequent phases of the sector's development would reveal, policymakers' approach to tackling hawker-related challenges would not change much, concentrating on similar tropes of furthering hawker legislation and enforcement of hawker operations.

Conclusion

Hawking in Singapore flourished during the colonial era, encouraged by waves of Chinese and Indian immigration into Singapore. This spike in hawker numbers was stimulated by two socioeconomic drivers, the first being hawking's appeal as a transitory vocation that many could quickly undertake in times of structural and frictional unemployment, and the second the need to meet high demand for affordable and convenient food, providing an essential service to labourers who did not have time or the means to cook their own food. As Singapore's population grew, so did hawking and its concomitant public health and urban pollution problems. Initial attempts to address this were piecemeal, with legislation underdeveloped and hawker shelters insufficient. At times, this culminated in unsuccessful attempts at eradicating the trade altogether. A shift in attitudes came in 1932, when the administration recognised the importance of hawkers to the port city and sought to retain the trade whilst managing hawking-related problems. However, attempts at addressing these issues through licensing and shelters remained more rhetorical than substantive, with the authorities lacking proper policymaking and enforcement capabilities to effect real change.

Chapter 5
Phase 2: Hawking during World War II and Post-War Singapore (1942 to 1965)

{O}

World War II (WWII) and the years leading to Singapore's independence were some of the country's most formative years. The war had plunged the island into extended economic depression, with many people finding new ways to survive during the Japanese Occupation and after. Singapore's post-war recovery and transition to an independent republic, which spanned two decades, profoundly transformed its economic and social fabric, with significant implications for both the nation and its residents. Against this backdrop, the second phase of hawking began, categorised by a rapid uptick in hawking and the exacerbation of hawking-related issues. It is here, in Phase 2, that one is better able to appreciate both the full extent of the hawking problem and the reasons why so many turned to hawking.

This chapter is shaped by a few cornerstone questions: What was Singapore's hawking scene like during WWII? How did it grow and evolve after the war? Why did hawkers stay in the trade after the war, and how did the administration respond to this growth in hawker numbers? To this end, we will first discuss how hawkers persevered through the war (1942–1945). Although documentation from this period is scarce, oral accounts can give us an insight into what the trade was like. Subsequently, we will explore the uptick in hawking in post-war Singapore (1945–1965) and how government policy evolved in response to these changes.

Hawkers and Hawking during World War II

On 15 February 1942, Singapore fell to the Imperial Japanese Army. Lieutenant-General Arthur Percival surrendered the Straits Settlement to Tomoyuki Yamashita, a Japanese army commander. This marked the beginning of the Japanese Occupation, changing the lives of the local population. The occupiers imposed a variety of measures to assimilate the locals into the Japanese way of life, including mandatory learning of the Japanese language and culture. The war years were characterised by pervasive monitoring and policing, with locals living in constant fear of persecution.

The war was a severe shock to Singapore's food system. Supply lines from Japan, Europe, Burma and Thailand were disrupted, affecting the import of non-perishables, consumables and the local production of foodstuffs such as tofu, bread, biscuits and confectionery.[1] Meeting basic needs became a challenge for the local population, who were forced to come up with innovative ways to get around shortages. Substitutes were used in place of common ingredients, such as tapioca flour in place of wheat or rice flour when making noodles. To cope with the food shortages, 'Peace Living Certificates' (see Figure 5.1) or ration cards were used to distribute food amongst the populace. Rations were allocated according to family sizes, but quantities often fell short of families' needs.

The shortages resulted in the trading of food items on the black market as well as food price inflation. In an attempt to address this issue, the Japanese implemented price controls on groceries, with daily price updates published in the newly established national newspaper *The Syonan Times*. Although the food situation during the occupation years did not reach famine levels, malnutrition and hunger were rampant and poignantly visible amongst the citizenry.

Despite the political and economic instability, hawking continued throughout the war years. In some odd cases, hawker businesses even

Figure 5.1.   Peace Living Certificate (1942)

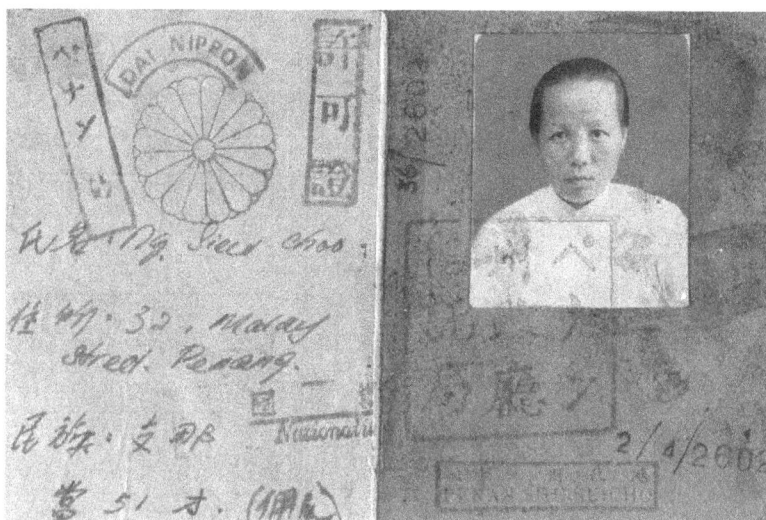

Source: Chew Chang Lang Collection, courtesy of National Archives of Singapore.

thrived. Hawking was conducted in a similar fashion to Phase 1, with unlicensed, itinerant basket and pushcart hawkers roaming the streets and selling simple fare. Unfortunately, little official documentation pertaining to hawkers during the wartime years has been preserved, leaving us with little substantive evidence to illuminate what hawker culture was like during the occupation. What we do have, however, are oral accounts from hawkers themselves, giving us a glimpse into what hawking might have been like during the war.

The first account we have is from Wong Hiong Boon, who was then a teenager living with his parents.[2] Wong recounts his time as an itinerant hawker, going door-to-door from the fifth-mile to seventh-mile area (near present-day Serangoon and Hougang) selling steamed rice cakes. The rice cakes were made by his mother every morning, which Wong would carry around in a wooden rattan basket to sell. On occasion, he would head out with his schoolmates, each carrying their own basket of cakes. Hawking often started after lunch and concluded right before dinner time. Rice cakes were sold at two cents apiece, and Wong would carry around 50 pieces each time. If business was good that day, Wong would come back home for a refill before going back out again. His story is perhaps emblematic of most itinerant hawkers at the time, with the hawking scene fuelled by simple acts of entrepreneurship in the hopes of supplementing family incomes.

Another account comes from Lu Yaw, a teacher and associate of the businessman and philanthropist Tan Kah Kee.[3] According to Lu, working in the education sector as a middle-aged Chinese man made him the subject of heavy scrutiny by the occupying forces. Many in similar professions were at risk of being detained by the *Kempetai* (the Japanese military police) on suspicion of having links to the Chinese intellectual movement, as the Japanese looked to purge anti-Japanese movements in Chinese-majority countries and Chinese intellectuals such as students or teachers were high on the Kempetai's watchlist. To disassociate himself and his students from the intellectual movement, Lu and his students would moonlight as hawkers. After school, instead of returning home, they would hawk on the streets, selling snacks such as *you char kway* (fried dough sticks), masking their statuses as Chinese intellectuals.

A third account comes from Jean and Dawn Yip, third-generation descendants of a pushcart hawker business known as Yip Kee Chicken Porridge Stall.[4] The stall was first started by their grandmother on Bugis Street in the 1940s, not long before the war. They sold Guangdong-style porridge, with their father helping in the shop before taking over the business after the war. The Yip sisters recounted stories they heard from their grandmother, who shared that business was so good that they were always busy, at times selling 60 chickens a day. This was so even during the war; thus, the Yips managed to avoid hunger as they owned a successful business and had ready access to food. Given the popularity of the shop, her grandmother had to hire assistants to run the stall, offering free meals in return for their work.

These accounts suggest that Singapore's hawker scene persisted despite the war and tough living conditions. Hawking grew into a multifaceted phenomenon, with many turning to it as a means of supplementing their income and ameliorating the effects of unemployment. For others, hawking had a secondary effect of masking a potentially sensitive identity. Both itinerant hawkers (such as Wong) and pushcart hawkers (like Yip Kee Porridge) were prevalent, with some even thriving throughout the war. Given the dearth of employment opportunities during the war years, these stories are emblematic of the durability and entrepreneurial spirit of hawkers, demonstrating the socioeconomic necessity of the trade as well as its potential even in dire times.

Post-War Rebuilding

The war severely disrupted Singapore's economy and development, and the British government's main focus after the end of the occupation was the country's post-war recovery. As in wartime, faced with economic depression and limited job opportunities, many turned to hawking to get by, with hawker numbers growing in tandem with the population. Across Singapore's history, the 'hawker problem' was most prominent during this period.

At its peak, the number of hawkers grew by 46%, increasing from around 12,000 in 1931 to 30,000 in 1947, before shrinking slightly to around 25,000 hawkers in 1950. Hawker population density — the percentage of the population working as hawkers — was at an all-time high at 3.17% in 1947 and 2.46% in 1950 (see Table 5.1). To put these numbers into perspective, Singapore's 1979 post-hawker reform hawker population density was 0.58%, almost a fifth of the 1950 numbers. Although we do not have specific annual numbers, the

Table 5.1.   Population to Hawker Ratio (1931, 1947, 1950)

Year	Hawkers	Population	Hawker Population Density	Phase of Hawking
1931	12,000	562,866	2.17%	Phase 1
1947	29,764	938,144	3.17%	Phase 2
1950	25,000	1,015,453	2.46%	

Note: Numbers for 1931 are for licensed hawkers. Numbers for 1947 onwards include both licensed and unlicensed hawkers. It should be noted that the number of licensed hawkers was most likely underreported, given the largely transient and itinerant nature of the trade at the time.

Source: Ryan Kueh 2024. Compiled from Straits Settlement Annual Report 1951, 73; Hawkers Inquiry Commission 1950, 68–69; Report of the Committee Appointed to Investigate the Hawker Question in Singapore, 1931, 204–205.

relatively high hawker population density likely remained through the 1950s, buoyed by the economy's slow post-war recovery.[5] By 1966, the hawker population had grown to around 45,000, but hawker population density remained roughly unchanged at 2.33%.[6]

The ballooning hawker population prompted the City Council to form a commission to investigate. The resulting report, known as the *Report of the Hawkers Inquiry Commission (1950)*, provided vital insights into hawkers' motivations through extensive surveys and observations, something the 1932 Committee did not achieve. Notable members of the commission include Dr. Thomas Henry Silcock, a professor at the University of Malaya, and Lim Yew Hock, who would eventually become Chief Minister of Singapore.

The 1950 Report described hawkers as "primarily a public nuisance to be removed from the streets,"[7] where hawkers were the "biggest retarding factor in the department's unremitting efforts to clean up the congested areas or the town."[8] Like before, hawkers were seen as the chief contributors to hygiene and spatial issues in the city, with many found operating with inadequate equipment and supplies of clean water to keep utensils free from infection. Further, hawkers had little education and were resistant to the authorities' attempts to clean up. According to the Commission,

> "...[t]hey have absolutely no respect for law or order, they not only completely obstruct the streets with their paraphernalia and stock-in-trade in the most populous areas of the town, causing serious difficulties to street cleansing and obstruction to pedestrian and wheeled traffic, but litter the streets with decomposed foodstuffs and refuse of all sorts."[9]

In addition to the restiveness of hawkers, their mobility, anonymity and the sheer scale of the trade added to the challenges of regulating the sector.

Drivers of Hawking in Post-War Singapore

The Commission attributed the rise in hawker numbers to a combination of economic, social and political factors. Economically and socially, the post-war landscape brought about chronic unemployment, with the situation worsened by a growing population.[10] Singapore's population continued growing despite the war, with the now-impoverished society further driving demand for affordable food options and contributing to the stickiness of hawking. This created a tense political situation where, on the one hand, a weak state and post-war conditions encouraged a rise in hawking, which itself inadvertently posed obstacles to the recovering city's public health and urban planning efforts. On the other hand, hawking was widely understood, supported, and even taken up by the public themselves. Solving the hawker problem was thus a fine line the colonial administration had to tread.

Of the three factors, the weak economy was the most salient driver. The Commission itself noted that "hawking is a result of unemployment and economic distress…to provide an alternative means of livelihood in the event of such disasters are merest common sense."[11] Many joined the trade not because they wished to be hawkers per se but because it

Figure 5.2. Reasons for Hawking (1950)

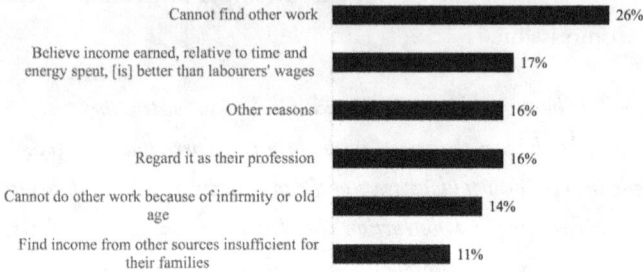

Note: Point 6 is awkwardly phrased, but kept to remain true to the report. Alternatively: "hawking as a supplementary income stream as current sources of income are insufficient to support their family."
Source: Ryan Kueh 2024. Compiled from Hawkers Inquiry Commission 1950, 10.

was an economically sensible and necessary decision. The Commission identified three main phenomena that propelled the uptake of the trade: First, there was a lack of economic opportunities and jobs after the war. Figure 5.2 compiles a list of reasons for hawking, with the inability to find other work cited as the primary reason (26% of respondents). 50% of surveyed hawkers began hawking after the end of the war in 1945, 20% began hawking during the war itself and the remaining 30% were longstanding hawkers.[12] This means that approximately 12,500 hawkers picked up the trade in the five years after the war, accounting for the meteoric rise in hawker numbers.[13]

Second, hawking was an accessible vocation that had low barriers to entry. Due to the low education and skill levels of the post-war citizenry, which made it difficult to access other skilled jobs, many turned to hawking. From the sampled range of hawkers, 57% of hawkers were unable to read or write in any of the four principal languages (English, Mandarin, Malay, Tamil), and less than 1% of respondents were able to read or write in English.[14] As such, it would have been difficult for hawkers to attain administrative jobs within the colonial administration or skilled jobs that required the ability to read or write.

Third, for the unskilled and lowly-educated, hawking provided a better income than the other jobs available to them. We know this from comparing the average daily net incomes of hawkers to the daily-rated salaries of jobs available in the market. Figure 5.3a shows us the specific breakdown of hawkers' daily net incomes. 35% of hawkers reported a daily net income of less than $2, 43% of hawkers said they made $2 to $4 per day, and 11% of hawkers took home $4 to $5. This amounts to over 65% of hawkers reporting a daily net income of $2 or more. Only two surveyed hawkers (1%) reported a loss.

Comparing this to a sample of daily-rated wages from the 1951 Straits Settlements Annual Report (see Figure 5.3b),[15] we see that the average daily net income of hawkers was generally higher than other potential jobs available to the low-skilled or low-educated at the time.[16] Although the range of a hawker's potential net income varied more, meaning that hawkers could risk earning less than other daily-rated jobs, hawking would still have been a comparable or better source of income. Not only did hawking have better earning potential compared with most labourers' daily wages, but it was also relatively easier and safer than

Figure 5.3a.   Surveyed Net Income of Hawkers (1950)

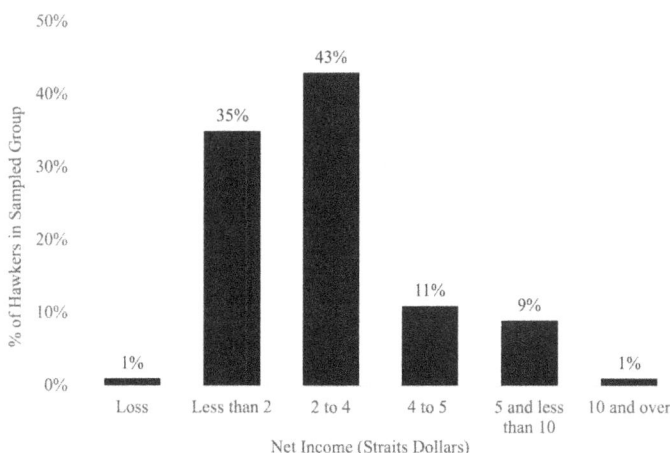

Source: Ryan Kueh 2024. Compiled from Hawkers Inquiry Commission 1950, 71.

Figure 5.3b.   Comparison of Hawking Net Income with Daily Wages
(1950–1951)

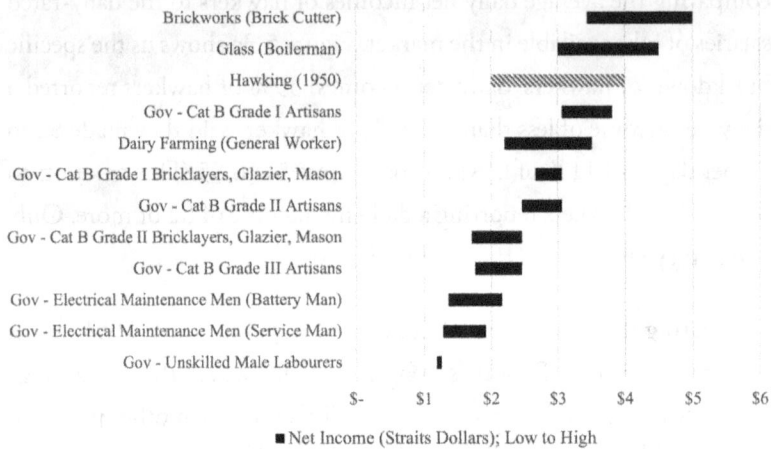

■ Net Income (Straits Dollars); Low to High

Source: Ryan Kueh 2024. Compiled from Hawkers Inquiry Commission 1950, 71; Straits Settlements Annual Reports 1951, 30–39.

other blue-collar jobs that were labour-intensive and potentially dangerous (e.g., brick cutter or boilerman). Given these considerations, hawking was a pragmatic choice.

Complementing the rise in hawker supply was robust public demand for hawker food. The Commission estimated that hawkers and licensed eating houses served an average of 375,000 customers per day, which amounted to 37% of the population.[17] In suburban areas, licensed eating houses and coffeeshops served an average of 278 daily customers per shop, with numbers reaching as high as 1,300. This demand was even higher for shops around the business district (Empress Place, Malacca Street, Market Street, Finlayson Green) which supported an average of 550 daily customers in 1951. The 1950 Commission was the first time a study on hawker demand was conducted, so we have no data with which to compare demand between the wartime and post-war periods.

Nevertheless, these numbers show us the importance of hawkers in servicing a large portion of the populace with affordable food.

In sum, the uptick of hawking during Phase 2 was informed by poor post-war macroeconomic conditions, compounded by Singapore's population growth since Phase 1 despite the war. The 1950 Commission found empirical evidence to support the motivations behind hawking, with a lack of other opportunities, the accessibility of hawking and better earning potential forming the main reasons for undertaking the vocation. This allowed hawking to exist as a 'self-help' mode of staying afloat for the uneducated and unskilled. These drivers, coupled with a poor economic recovery, continued to undergird the hawking phenomenon through the 1950s and early 1960s, contributing to the growing hawker population and hawker-related problems until Singapore's independence.

Post-War Attempts at Hawking Policy and Control

Faced with a war-torn economy, a weak state and a growing hawker population, Singapore's colonial administrators had a huge task ahead of them. On the one hand, hawkers played an important role in assisting the city's economic recovery, providing the working class with affordable food and keeping people in employment. On the other hand, growing hawker numbers exacerbated public health concerns and urban planning issues, contributing to the difficulty of Singapore's post-war recovery. In response, the 1950 Commission introduced three long-term policy recommendations that were imperative in setting the strategic direction for Singapore's hawker policy through Phases 2 and 3.

The first recommendation was to codify the necessity of hawkers within policy, with the Commission taking the view that the trade should be *permanently* retained. They wrote:

> "...[Policy] should not be directed toward eliminating hawking entirely, even as a long-term policy. Many of the underlying causes favouring

hawking in Singapore are likely to persist. It may be desirable to try to educate the public as buyers in the direction of more hygienic buying; but it is by no means certain that hawkers should be totally prohibited."[18]

This was an important departure of principle from the earlier administration, which had maintained, and at times supported, the possibility that hawkers should be completely eradicated, with staunch support coming from the Town Cleansing Department.[19] The reason for this departure is unclear. However, one possible motive was the colonial administration wanting to align larger administrative goals with local views in preparation for Singapore's limited self-governance. The 1953 Rendel Commission, which took place soon after the 1950 Commission, gave Singapore limited self-government and allowed Singaporeans to have domestic elections insofar as the British retained control over internal security and foreign affairs.[20] Interestingly, Lim Yew Hock, Singapore's Chief Minister between 1956 to 1959, was part of both the 1950 Hawkers Inquiry Commission and the 1953 Rendel Commission.

The second long-term recommendation was the proposed installation of 'permanent hawker shelters'. These permanent shelters differed from the fixed-pitched hawker shelters previously used in Phase 1, which were stalls that housed hawkers in a temporary location but could be moved if needed. By contrast, these permanent shelters were meant to integrate into the city's larger urban planning and agglomerate hawkers within key residential and commercial areas, although the Commission did not say how many they planned to build or where. Aside from providing basic cleaning facilities, the planned permanence of these proposed shelters demanded greater consideration of shelter locations and alignment with wider urban planning, which was to be decided by a permanent hawker advisory board. To incentivise the uptake of these new shelters, the Commission further recommended that hawkers within these government-sanctioned shelters should have their rents subsidised.[21]

The third long-term recommendation promoted upskilling, where the Commission advocated for assistance to be given to hawkers who wished to change their occupation and learn a new trade. This policy would funnel hawkers away from the trade, allowing them to be permanently and gainfully employed in industries that would contribute to Singapore's recovery.

Before these long-term recommendations could be implemented, however, the government first had to institute some level of control over the hawker population. This informed the Commission's short-term recommendations, which focused on establishing control through the licensing and monitoring of hawkers. To do this, the Commission reiterated the continuation of the licensing scheme (similar to Phase 1) except with more stringent enforcement, and recommended the establishment of a hawker-specific department to accomplish this.

Licensing was seen as the most effective method of regulating the hawker sector. Subjecting hawkers to administrative oversight would enable the bureaucratisation and formalisation of the hawking trade. In the Commission's view,

> "the only way to overcome this evil is once more to make the license a permit which is regarded as real and valid, and to inculcate the habit of obeying regulations, however limited, merely because they are the legal condition of the license and because those who obey are unmolested while the small minority that disobeys is severely punished."[22]

The Commission pursued several policy recommendations to this effect, such as mandating registration and signage displays. Under that latter policy, it stipulated that cooked food hawkers had to create and display signs associated with their stalls. Hawkers often named their stalls after the street they were on or their own names (e.g., Albert Street Beef Ball Noodles, Kim's Famous Hokkien Mee), a practice that has endured until today.[23]

Complementing the focus on licensing was the recommendation for a hawker-specific department within the government. The Commission proposed setting up a permanent hawker advisory board to focus on the routine management of hawkers and establish offices tasked specifically with creating, managing and enforcing hawker-related policies.[24] This included introducing hawker inspectors whose main job was to police and enforce hawker-related policies, with a ratio of one inspector for every 2,000 to 3,000 hawkers. Hawker inspectors would also be given the authority to summon hawkers for hygiene or licensing infractions.[25] The Commission viewed the establishment of health inspectors as important, as they would exist as agents of the state that were not the police but were nonetheless sufficiently empowered to enforce hawker-related legislation. This would allow the administration to enforce policies and correctional legislation without riling the public, for it was "politically unhealthy that the police, for a relatively trivial reason, should be driven to frequent use of force against a group of people who command wide public sympathy."[26]

Reality of Recommendations

In reality, the administration was slow to adopt the Commission's recommendations into policy, and even slower to enforce them. The short-term licensing recommendation was not implemented until 1954, four years after the report, and the establishment of the Markets and Hawkers Department (MHD) was delayed until 1957.[27] The MHD, Singapore's first hawker-specific bureaucratic arm housed under the Ministry of Health's Public Health Division, was an amalgamation of both the permanent hawker advisory board and the hawker inspector force. Despite these developments, the administration was unable to resolve the hawker problem. In fact, the number of illegal hawkers continued to grow, going from 25,000 in 1950 to over 30,000 by 1959.[28] With only 16 inspectors to monitor some 30,000 hawkers, enforcement lacked both teeth and resources, and the MHD was unable to effectively implement both short- and long-term recommendations.

Given the large numbers of illegal hawkers and the MHD's administrative deficiencies, the government began using the police to crack down on the growing unlicensed hawker population. This was despite the Commission's previous warnings and awareness of its political repercussions, and the progressively harsher crackdowns drew equally harsh responses from hawkers. Tensions between hawkers and authorities reached a point where J. Ephraim, then the chief of the City Cleansing Department declared "war" on unlicensed hawkers, proclaiming that the department would "prosecute these stubborn unlicensed hawkers' day and night until they give in."[29] The hard-line approach damaged trust between the administration and hawkers, with hawkers turning to secret societies and gangs for protection.[30] From the hawkers' perspective, agreeing to the administration's bureaucratic demands would have been a negative compromise, as mandatory licensing fees and moving into permanent shelters would have affected footfall and reduced potential business. Furthermore, complying with legislation, such as being licensed, meant that hawkers were at risk of prosecution under the new laws, introducing more inconvenience and potential penalties compared to just operating as an illegal hawker. The 1950 Commission's recommendations were thus largely ineffective within this phase. By 1966, hawker numbers had grown another 15,000 to an estimated 45,000, with fixed-pitched hawker shelter occupancy at 25% — or "practically empty".[31]

Conclusion

Hawking in post-war Singapore (Phase 2) marked the height of the 'hawker problem' in its history, featuring some of the highest hawker numbers and hawker population densities across the three phases. Hawking surged after World War II, with almost 50% of hawkers, numbering around 12,500 individuals, picking up the trade after the war. A slow economic recovery further accentuated the stickiness of hawking, incentivising more to enter or remain in the trade and pushing up public demand for hawker food. In response to these problems, the British administration sought to better understand what drew people to the trade, with the 1950 Commission uncovering watershed findings pertaining to hawkers' motivations. It found that hawking was mainly an economic problem, where lack of opportunities, low barriers to entry and relatively good earning potential were the three main reasons for undertaking the vocation. The Commission's policy recommendations, however, unfortunately had more bark than bite, and their slow and weak implementation made it difficult to effect any substantive change on the hawker problem. But ultimately, as we will see in the next chapter, these policy recommendations were indeed a step in the right direction, coming to form the basis of Singapore's hawker reform after independence.

Chapter 6
Phase 3: Independent Singapore and Hawker Reform, Part One (1965 to 1969)

𝕀𝕆𝕀

In 1965, Singapore separated from the Federation of Malaysia. This sudden change in circumstance and loss of its natural resource hinterland brought about an acute awareness of the newly independent country's vulnerabilities, forcing the ruling People's Action Party (PAP) to look for alternative development strategies.[1] Their "immediate concern after independence was the very viability of the island's 'survival' … [as Singapore was] still a non-industrialized economy with a high rate of underemployment and unemployment plus a high birth rate."[2] In a bid to develop the new nation, the PAP implemented extensive social, economic and political reforms, with a focus on rapid economic development and social reform. Hawkers were not spared from this, with the hawker industry being reshaped along the broader economy.

In this examination of the third phase of hawking (1965 to present), we will explore the PAP government's hawker reforms, which spanned a four-year period from 1969 to 1973. Unlike the ineffective hawker control policies of the colonial and pre-independence administrations, PAP governance marked a turning point for rampant illegal hawking. Policies directed at reforming the hawking landscape were initiated in 1969, and further policies were progressively introduced, ultimately solving the 'hawker problem' by 1973. Broadly speaking, the government retained similar strategies and instruments as the previous administrations (Phases 1 and 2) but yielded exponentially better results. One key difference that undergirded the success of the administration was *state strength*. State strength refers to the increased bureaucratic power and state capacity the PAP built to enact socio-economic reforms, including but not limited to hawker reform. Drawing on increased state strength, the government actively disincentivised the trade, nudging many away from the industry whilst simultaneously enforcing structures of formalisation — licensing of hawkers, better hygiene conditions and spatial agglomeration — that shaped the hawking industry into what it is today.

Within four years, the government managed to achieve the first significant reduction in hawker numbers, with hawker population density falling to 1.83% in 1969, the first time it had dropped below 2% in Singapore's recorded history. Table 6.1 and Figure 6.1 provide a comparison of gross hawker populations and hawker population densities across the three phases. From 1966 to 1974, as the general population grew by 15.3% from 1.93 million to 2.23 million, the government reduced hawker population density by 59% from 2.33% to 0.95%, with hawker population density continuing to decrease through the late 1970s. This decrease is associated with expanding economic opportunities, which fundamentally changed the incentives for joining or remaining in hawking (see Figure 6.2). Hawkers left the trade for better job opportunities, facilitated by active government intervention that redirected hawkers into other productive industries.

This necessitates a deeper understanding of hawker policy during the critical first decade post-independence. Why did addressing the hawker problem carry economic and political salience? How did the PAP become the first government to successfully address the 'hawker problem' without political blowback? What forces supported this? This chapter will provide a comprehensive breakdown of Phase 3 of Singapore's hawker reform, looking at why and how the PAP government changed the hawking industry. Given the complexity of the reforms, this section will be split into two parts. Broadly, Chapter 6, which covers Part One, will focus

Table 6.1. Total Population of Hawkers alongside Population (1931 to 1978)

Year	Hawker Population	Total Population	Hawker Population Density	Phase of Hawking
1931	12,000	562,866	2.13%	Phase 1
1947[3]	29,764	938,144	3.17%	Phase 2
1950	25,000	1,015,453	2.46%	
1966	45,000	1,934,400	2.33%	Phase 3
1967	43,289*	1,977,600	2.19%	
1968	40,336*	2,012,000	2.00%	
1969	37,436*	2,042,500	1.83%	
1970	34,785*	2,074,507	1.68%	
1971	32,543*	2,112,900	1.54%	
1972	31,030*	2,152,400	1.44%	
1973	22,335**	2,193,000	1.02%	
1974	21,179	2,229,800	0.95%	
1975	19,700	2,262,600	0.87%	
1976	17,641	2,293,300	0.77%	
1977	15,588	2,323,530	0.67%	
1978	13,763	2,353,600	0.58%	

*Author's estimates
**Year of Final 'extensive hawker control programme' by the Hawkers Department

Source: Ryan Kueh 2024. Compiled from Straits Settlement Annual Report 1951, 73; Hawkers Inquiry Commission 1950, 68–69; Ministry of Environment/Hawkers Department (HD) Annual Report 1971–1973, 11; Ministry of Environment/Hawkers Department (HD) Annual Report 1959–1970; Ministry of Environment/Hawkers Department (HD) Statistics on Hawker Licences 1979, 2–3, 46, 53–63, 120, 210, 270; Report of the Committee Appointed to Investigate the Hawker Question in Singapore 1931, 204–205; Yong 1966, 1; World Bank, retrieved 2023.

on the *why* of hawker reform, exploring the reasons that necessitated the PAP addressing the hawker issue and providing supporting political context. Chapter 7, which covers Part Two, will focus on the *how* of hawker reform, including the instruments and specific policies used to restructure the industry.

Figure 6.1.   Hawker Population Densities from 1931 to 1978

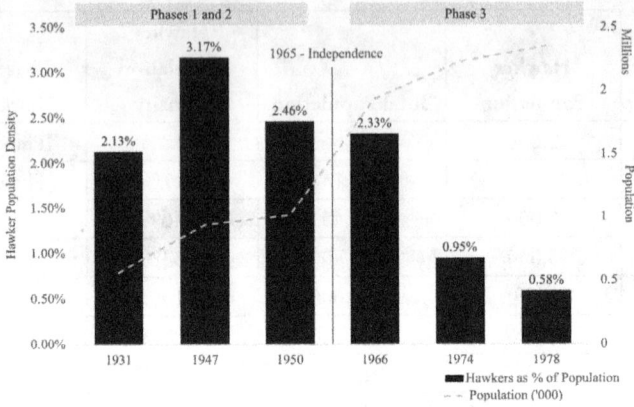

Note: Before 1966 Unlicensed, After 1966 Licensed.

Source: Ryan Kueh 2024. Compiled from Report of the Committee Appointed to Investigate the Hawker Question in Singapore 1931, 204–205; Straits Settlement Annual Report 1951, 73; Hawkers Inquiry Commission 1950, 68–69; Ministry of Environment/Hawkers Department (HD) Annual Report 1971–1973, 11; Ministry of Environment/Hawkers Department (HD) Statistics on Hawker Licences 1979, 2–3, 46, 53, 63, 120.

Figure 6.2.   Hawker Population Density and GDP Growth (1966–1978)

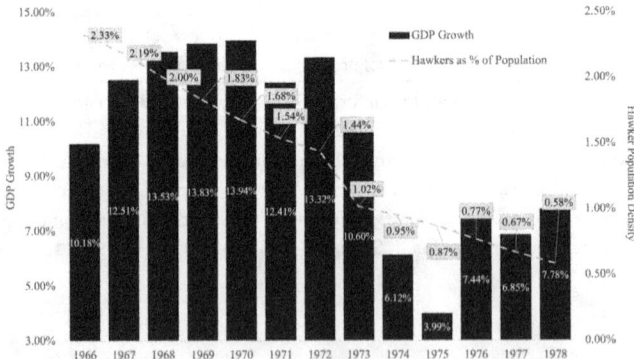

Source: Ryan Kueh 2024. Compiled from Straits Settlement Annual Report 1951, 73; Hawkers Inquiry Commission 1950, 68–69; Ministry of Environment/Hawkers Department (HD) Annual Report 1971–1973, 11; Ministry of Environment/Hawkers Department (HD) Statistics on Hawker Licences 1979, 2–3, 46, 53, 63, 120; World Bank, retrieved 2023; World Bank & OECD, retrieved 2023.

Economic and Political Salience of the Hawker Problem

With around 45,000 hawkers by the beginning of Phase 3, the 'hawker problem' needed to be urgently addressed. Rampant illegal hawking had severe economic and political ramifications. It presented an obstacle to the PAP's reform strategy, one that focused on restructuring the economy away from entrepôt trade to a broad-based economy built on manufacturing, oil refining, financing and services by developing Singapore's human capital through education and upskilling.[4] Hawkers posed a threat to this strategy, one that can be understood in economic and political terms.

In economic terms, illegal hawkers deprived the state of human capital to fuel its industrial growth. Hawking was perceived as a low-productivity occupation that "directly competed with the expanding manufacturing sector for labour."[5] Every hawker on the street meant one less worker that could be upskilled or employed in productive industry. The labour shortage endured through the 1970s and was particularly acute by the middle of the decade, driven by Singapore's swift industrialisation.[6] This persisted despite British withdrawal in 1971, which resulted in the retrenchment of 17,000 civilian employees, with the government relaxing immigration laws to grant work permits to non-citizens amid continued demand for labour.[7] Between 1966 to 1970, around 2.33% of the population (approximately 45,000 people in 1966) to 1.68% (approximately 34,785 people in 1970) were hawkers respectively, contributing to the labour shortage. To put this into perspective, hawker population density in 1978 was at 0.58% (13,763), meaning that approximately 31,000 workers transitioned into productive industry. Although it was unlikely that hawker diversion substantively resolved the labour shortage, addressing the hawker issue was an integral part of a wider nationwide effort to fuel Singapore's industrialisation.

Politically, unregulated hawking posed larger ancillary challenges to the administration. First, hawker governance was traditionally a hot-button issue through which political incumbents could gain or lose public trust, chipping away at the PAP's legitimacy the longer the hawker problem persisted. The number of hawkers served as a barometer of economic opportunity, a rough measurement of the population that felt economically and socially deprived. Hawker population density was a yardstick for the effectiveness of the incumbent's social and economic policies, as many only took to hawking as a stop-gap vocation. Thus, the more — and the longer — hawkers were on the streets, the more poorly this reflected on the economic policies of the incumbent, hurting political legitimacy and valence politics.

Second, as most hawkers operated on the fringes of the formal economy without licences or regulations, informal hawkers created a myriad of problems related to public health, spatial disorder and tax evasion, exacerbating the aforementioned challenges to the government's reform goals and political legitimacy. This prolonged the longstanding socio-political tension between hawkers and the state. Previously, attempts by the colonial government to discipline or regulate hawkers were interpreted as punishing the working class for their resourcefulness and restricting the supply of affordable food. This was most evident during Phases 1 and 2, where efforts to control the hawkers either by enforcement or eradication often triggered popular mobilisation against the colonial government.[8] For the PAP, addressing these problems was thus difficult, with the historically antagonistic colonial government setting the precedent for a tenuous government-hawker relationship.

The restiveness of hawkers posed a challenge to the legitimacy of the new government in multiple ways. Itinerant hawkers contributed to the perception of public disorder, which could disincentivise foreign investment. Alternatively, they suggested that the PAP government was not serious about reforming Singapore. Controlling the hawkers and reforming the hawker industry was thus an important task, with 'control' here referring to the state's ability to implement new policies relating to the hawker population, such that hawkers might be willing to cede their individual rights in the collective interest. In this regard, the colonial administrations struggled to control the hawkers, but unsurprisingly, early attempts by the PAP also encountered grassroots resentment.[9] Given the historical baggage of harsh crackdowns, hawkers were uncooperative and sometimes outrightly opposed to the policy efforts of the PAP. The new government was aware of the sensitivity surrounding the hawker issue, writing in 1974:

> "The government recognises the role hawkers play in the socioeconomic life of the country. Their retail trade has helped to keep the cost of living down especially for the middle- and lower-income sections of our population. Their increasing importance as a tourist attraction must also be considered. Any attempts, therefore, to eliminate this form of livelihood will inevitably antagonise not only the hawkers but the general public resulting in political repercussions."[10]

The PAP was thus faced with a balancing act: trying to solve the hawker problem without inciting widespread political backlash. However, it was aided in its efforts by high levels of political legitimacy and public trust — conditions that facilitated the acceptance and enforcement of hawker-specific policies, which will be discussed in Chapter 7.

Political Context of the Hawker Reform (1965 to 1973): Legitimacy and Trust

The PAP's success in hawker reform was supported by the political environment it operated in, including a strong public mandate. As the first independently elected government in Singapore, the PAP enjoyed widespread political legitimacy and high levels of public trust, conditions integral in enabling the government to address the hawker problem successfully. There were two reasons for this, the first being the PAP's post-colonial origins. Being the first independently elected party, the PAP had robust elite cohesion, party durability and unquestioned authority amongst the public — at least after 1961. Political scientists Steven Levitsky and Lucan Way observe that "successful liberation struggles tend to produce a generation of leaders with extraordinary legitimacy and unquestioned authority",[11] creating conditions for political trust in the newly independent government. Dan Slater further adds that this effect comes from the party's counterrevolutionary origins, understood as dominant parties who "collaborate with departing colonial powers to defeat leftist parties."[12] In other words, the context in which the PAP rose to power contributed to its high levels of legitimacy and authority, allowing the government to generate continuous electoral support insofar as they provided steady economic growth and public goods.

The second reason contributing to a high level of trust in the PAP and government policy was the party's grassroots approach to politics. The goal of a grassroots approach is to create a society that "consists of a mesh of traditional networks of face-to-face communities with shared purposes, values and collective memories".[13] In other words, it emphasises the need for political elites to work with and consult the general population when tackling political issues, achieved through regular interaction and relationship-building. Developing the grassroots served a dual purpose, explicitly contributing to community-based national development and implicitly organising the masses for political legitimacy and social stability. This can be seen from then-Prime Minister Lee Kuan Yew's visibility amongst the hawkers and the public, such as his walkabouts with hawkers (see Figures 6.3 and 6.4). Such frequent engagement with the community conveyed the message that the new government was actively involved in the daily lives and concerns of its citizens, building rapport between the new elites and the local community and enmeshing leaders in the fabric of daily life.

Figure 6.3.   Then-Prime Minister Lee Kuan Yew Stopping at a Street Hawker Stall during His Tour of Paya Lebar Constituency in 1963

Source: Ministry of Information and the Arts Collection, courtesy of National Archives of Singapore.

The government's political legitimacy grew concomitantly with its economic successes in the 1960s and 1970s. The PAP's fear of economic stagnation resulted in an obsession with economic growth at all costs,[14] with a new social contract established where the PAP promised economic growth and 'survival' in exchange for continuous political support.[15] From 1966 to 1973 — just before the final hawker clean-up operation — the government clocked an era of double-digit growth rates, providing convincing evidence to the public that the PAP was fulfilling its economic ambitions. On the back of this growing legitimacy, the PAP progressively developed a bureaucracy that featured a large state apparatus and power, whereby citizens traded social liberty for continued economic performance.[16] With no serious political opposition, the increasing, albeit conditional, long-term support of the people, a growing bureaucracy and continued economic growth, the PAP enjoyed

Figure 6.4.   Then-Prime Minister Lee Kuan Yew's Tour of a Hawker Centre at High Street Road in 1963

Source: Ministry of Information and the Arts Collection, courtesy of National Archives of Singapore.

a monopoly on state control and the ability to plan for long-term policies. This gave the government the necessary political mandate to tackle the sensitive 'hawker problem', where the public and hawkers both trusted that the government's policy was working for the benefit of the people, allowing the administration to effectively implement and enforce hawker-related policies such as licensing and relocation.

Foreshadowing of Hawker Reform

Signs of the government's intent to overhaul the hawker sector can be traced back to 8 December 1965. Then-President Yusof Bin Ishak said in an address to Parliament:

> "*The reorganisation and expansion of the Environmental Health Services, Public Cleansing, Anti-Mosquito Services and Hawkers Department are being taken in hand and initial measures for improvement of*

transport, equipment, enforcement of discipline and supervisors have commenced".[17]

The announcement signalled the government's intent to clean up aesthetically displeasing parts of Singapore, which included hawkers. Two months later, on 9 February 1966, then-Minister for Health Yong Nyuk Lin introduced a new *Hawkers Code*, a policy that set the principles for the trade in Singapore.[18] The code was a first, providing concrete assurances to hawkers and outlining the right to hawking as a livelihood conditional upon (1) not endangering public health; (2) not obstructing traffic; and (3) not contravening law and order. The code also made hawker licences non-transferable and personal to the holder, meaning hawkers could only register as sole proprietors, and their licences could not be inherited without approval from the authorities. Although the government's *approach* towards the trade did not change much from the City Council administration's (Phase 2), it signified the first entrenchment of principles within *policy*. Further, it differed from the City Council in its operational considerations, where the PAP recognised the need for greater enforcement capabilities within aesthetic and public-health related functions, signifying the government's understanding of the core drivers of the hawking issue.

Informing the new code was the *1966 Hawkers Department Annual Report*. The 1966 Report listed the same issues of hygiene, sanitation and spatial obstruction as its predecessors as aspects of the 'hawker problem' to tackle. It reiterated the recognition that hawking was driven by financial privation, as "a social problem in that people become hawkers through economic necessity."[19] The Report further stated that:

> *"...the problem increases correspondingly and it cannot be solved merely by prosecution, demolition or providing alternative sites, but it must depend upon gradual education of the hawkers to increase civic consciousness. The whole process will also provide alternative avenues of employment for such citizens."*[20]

This appraisal of the situation demonstrates how the Hawkers Department viewed the hawker problem as a social issue that demanded sensitivity and careful policy calibration, a perspective that would come to be crucial in the development and enforcement of later hawker-related policies.

Another signal of hawker reform came in 1968 with the Keep Singapore Clean Campaign (KSCC). Described as the "sterilisation of Singapore",[21] the campaign sought to clean up aesthetically displeasing parts of the country and instil social education and discipline in the public. The campaign pushed for new public health laws, proper sewage system development, disease control and the relocation of itinerant hawkers, in the hopes that the clean-up would enhance the quality of life for Singaporeans and attract foreign investment.[22] At the inauguration of the KSCC in 1968, then-Prime Minister Lee Kuan Yew remarked that it was

> "...*necessary to meet greater pressures of higher densities of population, more housing estates, greater consumption of preserved and packaged foods leaving more domestic waste, and more hawkers in public places. We must create a public awareness of everyone's duty to keeping [sic] Singapore clean.*"[23]

Although this campaign was aimed at the Singaporean public in general, illegal and itinerant hawkers were one of its key target groups.

Conclusion

In this chapter, we discussed Singapore's political context from 1965 to 1969 prior to the PAP's hawker reforms, and why the 'hawker problem' was an important issue to tackle. First, hawkers posed threats to the new nation which needed to be addressed urgently. Economically, hawkers deprived other sectors of much-needed human capital, a low-productivity occupation that competed with productive industry for labour. Politically, the 'hawker problem' was a barometer of the new government's effectiveness in imposing regulatory and social reforms, in the sense that the longer the hawker problem persisted, the more poorly it reflected on the PAP government. Hawkers also constantly challenged the government for public space. Altogether, these threats made the hawker problem an urgent issue for the PAP to solve, informing the subsequent haste and conviction of their reforms. Second, the PAP government enjoyed a higher level of public trust given its post-colonial origins, with this legitimacy furthered through its grassroots approach and years of double-digit economic growth. This informed the social contract between the PAP and the public, with the citizenry willing to trade social liberty and political support in exchange for continued economic growth, giving the PAP the necessary political mandate to tackle the hawker problem. Lastly, signs of the government's plans can be seen from multiple speeches, including in 1965 by then-President Yusof Bin Ishak, in 1966 with the *New Hawkers Code* and again in 1968 with the KSCC. These signalled the government's intent to reform the hawking landscape, which began soon after in 1969 through the introduction of a new agency that governed hawking operations.

Chapter 7
Phase 3: Independent Singapore and Hawker Reform, Part Two (1969 to 1973)

{O}

We now turn to the period between 1969 to 1973, referred to in this text as the 'hawker reform' for ease. These were the years which saw the most extensive developments related to hawker control. From the previous chapters, we know that there was a lack of hawker-specific policies and substantive enforcement in Phases 1 and 2, throughout Singapore's time as a British colony, its years under Japanese occupation and its final pre-independence years. Hawker control took a drastic turn in Phase 3, with the new People's Action Party (PAP) government building legal, policy and operational strength to tackle the hawker problem.

Four bureaucratic instruments were crucial to the hawker reform. The first was the introduction of health- and food-specific laws that encompassed hawking operations, entrenched hygiene standards and social mores in legislation and laid the groundwork for hawker enforcement. The second instrument was a capacity-building push within the Hawkers Department ('the Department'), where the government focused on improving organisational and manpower capacity to facilitate the effective planning, licensing and enforcement of hawker-specific policies and legislation. The third instrument was the rapid roll-out of hawker centres, distinct from hawker shelters, with the government mandating the relocation of itinerant hawkers into hawker centres. The last instrument was hawker policy, which took a carefully calibrated, nuanced approach that paid heed to hawkers' own concerns.

This chapter has likewise been organised into four sections. First, we will touch on the specific legislation introduced to tackle the hawker problem. Second, we will discuss the growth of organisational capabilities within the Department. Third, we will examine the government's rapid construction of hawker centres and its efforts to relocate hawkers into these centres. Fourth, we consider hawker enforcement policy through the examples of licensing and relocation policy. Lastly, we turn to the final clean-up operation in 1973 that effectively brought an end to the 'hawker problem' in Singapore.

Instrument 1: Hawker-Related Legislation

The first arm of the hawker reform involved the implementation of new health and hygiene legislation governing hawker operations. These laws, such as the 1969 Environmental Public Health Act (EPHA) and the 1973 Sale of Food Act (SFA), sought to improve basic hygiene and cleanliness standards within Singapore, such that any infringement could constitute a criminal infraction.

The EPHA was the first piece of legislation to directly focus on improving Singapore's general hygiene standards by establishing a standardised code to govern health- and environment-related matters.[1] The EPHA mandated immunisation for food hawkers and required them to undergo proper food-handling training, such as educational courses on the preparation, storage and transport of food. Spatial restrictions were also introduced, prohibiting hawkers from setting up stalls within 45 metres of specified locations such as markets, schools, hospitals, clinics and police stations, in the hopes of reducing congestion around public amenities. Operationally, the EPHA integrated environmental health functions across the government into a single division. The second health-specific piece of legislation, the SFA, further tightened hygiene standards and placed a more stringent emphasis on food-specific hygiene. It added conditions and guidelines concerning the safe preparation of food for vendors, including hawkers, with non-compliance potentially resulting in a hefty fine or imprisonment of up to three months (see Figure 7.1).[2]

Figure 7.1. "Hawkers and the Health Law" Booklet (circa 1980s)

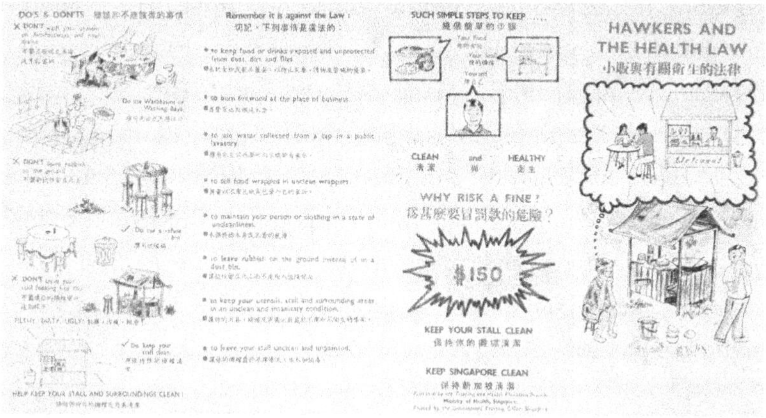

Source: Collection of the National Museum of Singapore, National Heritage Board.

These laws were novel for two reasons. First, the EPHA and SFA developed the young nation's first metrics for assessing hygiene standards and infringement. To test the food hygiene levels, the SFA introduced bacteria testing to ensure that food sold by hawkers was safe to consume. Further, hawkers now had to be hygiene-trained and educated, with infractions and punishments determined by the extent of deviation from the newly established hygiene standards. The EPHA and SFA added legislative clarity to punishments, where hawker infractions were now isolated and enforced based on the hawker's failure to uphold hygiene standards. This marked a departure from previous administrations, where infractions were punished on the basis of contributing to general public disorder rather than health-specific infractions.

Second, the EPHA empowered non-police health officers from the Department to punish hawkers for hygiene infractions. This was an actualisation of the 1950 Commission's recommendation, with the Department's health officers now legally empowered to impose fines on errant hawkers without a court hearing, effectively speeding up enforcement action. Selected public health inspectors (PHIs) such as Hawker Inspectors and Assistant Hawker Inspectors were allowed to impose penalties for health-related infractions. As PHIs were only authorised to take action regarding threats to public health, summonses from PHIs would be interpreted as offences against the public interest rather than crimes against the state. The usage of PHIs allowed the government to effectively enforce new hygiene rules without damaging public trust, with their limited authority constituting a type of 'neighbourhood policing'. Studies on neighbourhood policing have found that it helps to reduce public perceptions of disorder and increase trust and confidence in the enforcing authority, thereby increasing the authority's perceived legitimacy and improving problem-solving at a local level.[3]

Thus, the new government kickstarted the hawker reform in 1969 with the introduction of targeted hygiene legislation. Through the EPHA and SFA, the state not only established legally-binding hygiene standards but also provided a clear legal framework for hawker operations. These laws introduced metrics for assessing potential hygiene infractions and mandated hawker training and education. The EPHA empowered health inspectors to police hygiene infractions without damaging public trust in the authorities, streamlining enforcement actions and allowing officers to tackle the hawker problem efficiently and effectively. These new laws laid the foundation for state strength and provided the legal basis for effective policy enforcement whilst prioritising public health and trust. They also shifted the framing of hawker enforcement, creating an efficient yet politically and socially optimal vehicle for achieving this. Further, the usage of PHIs was an important departure from Phase 2, which attempted to use PHIs to carry out hawker enforcement but ultimately reverted to using the police when this failed. Coupled with a growth in the Department's manpower over the late 1960s and early 1970s (the second of the four instruments), these legislative developments were instantly effective. The number of hawkers- and market-related fines rose from 8,543 in 1969 to 14,641 in 1971, a 71% increase, while the number of hawkers continued to decrease from 1969 onwards.

Instrument 2: Organisational Capacity-Building within the Hawkers Department

The second instrument was the rapid build-up of the Department's planning and enforcement capabilities, which took place from 1965 to 1973. As seen from the previous phases of the hawker sector's development, even with the presence of laws and policies, a lack of operational capabilities on the part of the overseeing body contributed to repeated failures to regulate the sector. In 1958 (Phase 2), only 16 inspectors were monitoring some 30,000 hawkers.[4] For the new PAP government, enforcing its laws and policies against a growing number of unlicensed hawkers — some 45,000 by 1966 — was a monumental challenge. Learning from the mistakes of the previous administration, the Department scaled its enforcement capabilities to better match the sizeable hawker population. A larger inspector force would help to better facilitate the regulation of hygiene standards and spatial restrictions, encourage the adoption of good hawking practices and issue licences to unlicensed hawkers.

The growth of the Department's capabilities first began in 1966, with the number of public health enforcement officers more than doubling by 1973. Figure 7.2 below compiles the number of public health officials who presumably engaged in enforcement activities (collectively referred to as enforcement officers, or EOs) — Hawker Inspectors, Assistant Hawker Inspectors, Public Health Assistants and Public Health Overseers — based on the Department's annual reports between 1965 to 1973. It shows that in the years following independence, the Department's enforcement capabilities grew from 71 EOs in 1965 to 172 in 1973, with numerous vacancies remaining unfilled through the years.

This growth in EO numbers proved successful in making inroads with the licensing and control of hawkers. Between 1966 and 1972, unlicensed hawker numbers decreased from 45,000 to 31,030.[5] Table 7.1 contains estimates of the number of hawkers from 1967 to 1972, whilst

Figure 7.2.   Number of Enforcement Officers in the Hawkers Department

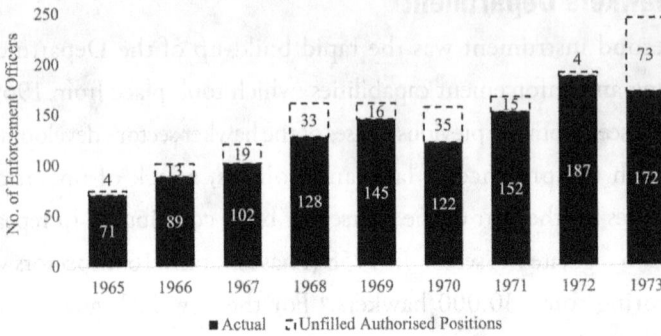

Source: Ryan Kueh 2024. Compiled from the Ministry of Environment/Hawkers Department (HD) Annual Reports between 1966–1973.

Table 7.1.   Total Number of New Hawker Licences Issued from 1967 to 1972

Year	Number of New Hawker Licences Issued
1967	1,711
1968	2,953
1969	2,900
1970	2,651
1971	2,242
1972	1,513
Total No. of Newly Licensed Hawkers	13,970

Note: The estimated number of unlicensed hawkers in 1966 was 45,000. By 1972, this number was recorded as 11,864. Deducting the number of new licences (13,970) issued from 1967 to 1972, this leaves a deficit of 19,166 hawkers unaccounted for.

Source: Ryan Kueh 2024. Author's estimates using number of annually licensed hawkers from the Annual Reports of the Ministry of Environment/Hawkers Department (HD) between 1959–1970s and Ministry of Environment/Hawkers Department (HD) Annual Report 1971–1973.

Figure 7.3 demonstrates a steady decline in unlicensed and licensed hawker numbers, which occurred in tandem with the Department's growth in enforcement capabilities. The numbers of unlicensed and licensed hawkers between 1967 and 1972 are estimates, derived by deducting the number of new licences issued from Health Minister Yong Nyuk Lin's 1966 hawker estimates and the Department's estimated number of unlicensed hawkers in 1972 (11,864).[6] This leaves us with

Figure 7.3.   Estimated Number of Unlicensed Hawkers between 1966 to 1972

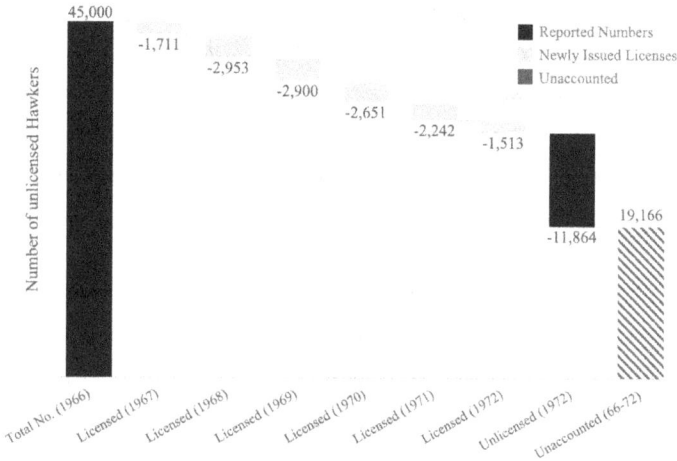

Source: Ryan Kueh 2024. Author's estimates using number of annually licensed hawkers from the Annual Reports of the Ministry of Environment/Hawkers Department (HD) between 1959–1970s and Ministry of Environment/Hawkers Department (HD) Annual Report 1971–1973.

19,166 hawkers unaccounted for; one possibility is that this group found jobs in other industries.

Clearly, the growth in enforcement capabilities between 1965 to 1973 had a general effect of reducing the number of unlicensed hawkers. A larger enforcement force would have facilitated licensing activity, alongside the enforcement of the new laws. Further, this period corresponds to Singapore's broader economic reforms, such that a combination of stronger enforcement and economic growth would have been strong drivers in turning hawkers away from the industry. This would be consistent with the theory that employment and positive economic conditions reduce the impetus to enter hawking.

In 1972, the Department further underwent organisational restructuring, expanding its capabilities to better facilitate its hawker policy planning and enforcement capabilities.[7] With the establishment of the Ministry of Environment in September 1972, the Department was transferred over from the Ministry of Health and placed under the purview of the new ministry's Environmental Public Health Division (EPHD).[8] This change of parent ministry provided an opportunity to reorganise the Department itself, with the intent of growing it into the second largest branch in the EPHD. The 1972 *Reorganisation of Hawker Branch* report mentions that the reorganisation was done in "recognition and reflection of the role of this branch in the context of the overall public health functions … [representative of the] short-term and long-term solutions and policy decisions that have to be evolved and implemented in the coming years".[9]

This reorganisation increased the scope of the Department's planning and enforcement capabilities, allowing the branch to introduce more specialised roles and develop long-term policies projecting seven to 10 years into the future. In 1973, the branch was segmented into four sections: Records and Licensing; Operations and Enforcement; Planning and Evaluation; and Administration,[10] with each section developing its own policies and carrying out its own operations. Given its larger size, the newly restructured branch required oversight from a higher-level officer. Both the then-Permanent Secretaries of the Ministry of Environment and the Ministry of Finance recommended that the branch be led by a "superscale G officer", the equivalent of a Deputy Secretary.[11] A larger and more specialised department would have allowed the Department to take on more ambitious projects that required inter-ministry coordination, enabling the effective operation of seminal policies such as the building of hawker centres and the final hawker clean-up operation in 1973.

In sum, the Department engaged in organisational capacity building that improved its ability to develop hawking policy, legislation and enforcement. This was done through a doubling of manpower from 1965 to 1973, with further enhancements after the 1972 restructuring. This signalled the government's growing public health enforcement capabilities as well as their bureaucratisation and specialisation, with the reorganisation better accommodating long-term policy planning and expanding organisational capabilities. By 1973, the Department had become a significant force, a powerful apparatus that would further enable hawker enforcement and reform.

Instrument 3: Hawker Centres and Permanence

The third key instrument was the swift construction of permanent and long-term, government-built shelters known as hawker centres. Despite successfully engaging in enforcement efforts, a solution was needed to permanently accommodate and ameliorate the hygiene and spatial problems associated with hawking. Moving vendors to a less crowded street is an easy but temporary solution, as if customers fail to follow, hawkers would have little choice but to return to their original locations.[12] Following the 1950 Commission's recommendation of long-term hawker shelters, hawker centres were redesigned hawker shelters that accompanied housing estates and community facilities. Hawker centres were first championed by the Ministry of Health in 1971, with this policy responsibility transferred over to the Ministry of Environment after the restructuring.[13] Similarly, the Ministry of Environment considered hawker centres a long-term solution to the hawker problem, with the intent of relocating all street hawkers into centralised buildings that would provide a "more efficient and ordered... collective groupings of hawkers in scheduled premises."[14]

Like their predecessor (hawker shelters), hawker centres fulfilled the primary functions of hygiene standardisation and spatial agglomeration. Within these centres, basic hygiene amenities such as washing and sanitation facilities, clean running water and waste disposal were provided by the state, increasing hygiene standards and reducing public health risks. Other common features of a hawker centre included high-roofed ceilings for ventilation, skylights to provide natural light and aid air circulation, air ducts over cooking areas and the provision of basic utilities such as electricity.[15] Spatially, hawker centres prevented crowds and congestion from accumulating on the streets, as most hawkers were only given licences to operate within the centres, effectively addressing the urban problems associated with itinerant hawkers. This centralisation also helped EOs perform routine hygiene compliance checks and disseminate hawker-related policies and information, educating hawkers on proper practices that elevated the sector overall. It also provided officers with a visual heuristic to identify unlicensed hawkers, as most other hawkers operating outside of hawker centres or night markets were likely to be illegal.

Compared with hawker shelters, hawker centres were novel in their public-focused design and *modus operandi*. First, hawker centres were designed alongside wider urban planning arrangements such as public housing. The intent was for the hawker centre to be a part of a holistic suite of public utilities, bringing the hawker's social utility to specific and sometimes under-served areas. This marked a shift in planning considerations, when previously, shelters were mainly designed to agglomerate hawkers within crowded areas only. Second, hawker centre design imposed operational discipline on hawkers. Before hawker centres, spaces located near specific hawker stalls were 'owned' by the respective hawkers, often leading to disputes between neighbouring hawkers (see Figure 7.4a). However, unlike hawker shelters, hawker centres came with infrastructure such as public chairs and tables that de-territorialised and de-privatised hawker culture (see Figure 7.4b). Such developments shifted the operational locus of control from the hawkers to the government, fundamentally changing how hawkers could operate (more in the next chapter). By imposing a measure of permanence and operational discipline on hawking, these changes helped to make the sector's operations more consistent and predictable, which in turn further facilitated better planning and enforcement.

The licensing of hawkers between 1966 to 1972 and the clean-up operation of 1973 meant that a significant number of hawkers required relocation. Hawker centres needed to be built at scale and speed as there were insufficient centres to accommodate the newly licensed hawkers, with *pasar malams* and temporary hawker shelters serving as interim locations (see Figure 7.5). The Ministry of Environment set a target of

Figure 7.4a.   Hawker Stalls at the Corner of Wayang Street in 1970 (Phase 2 of pre-reform hawking)

Source: Paul Piollet Collection, courtesy of National Archives of Singapore.

Figure 7.4b.   Tanglin Hawker Centre (1980; Phase 3 of post-reform hawking)

Source: Courtesy of the National Archives of Singapore.

Figure 7.5.   *Pasar Malam* (Night Market) at Smith Street and Trengganu Street (1965)

Source: Ministry of Information and the Arts Collection, courtesy of National Archives of Singapore.

relocating all hawkers into permanent hawker centres by 1975–1976, with the government planning for at least one hawker centre in every one of the constituencies (65 constituencies in 1972).[16] This meant that around 25–30 markets and centres had to be constructed each year for the next three to four years. Given this massive undertaking, intra-agency collaboration was central to this goal, with the Department working with multiple government agencies such as the Urban Renewal Department, Jurong Town Corporation, Public Works Department and other private agencies to construct the hawker centres.[17] By 1973, the Department had constructed 15 hawker centres, with more planned for or in the process of construction.[18]

Instrument 4: Hawker Policy

The efficiency of the new licensing and relocation policies can be attributed to good policy design. Policies accompanying or surrounding hawker reform were well-calibrated, complementing the work of other ministries surrounding economic reform. They were also sensitive to hawker-specific considerations, cushioning the impact of the reforms for hawkers and minimising political blowback.

A first example of good policy design was the linking of the hawker licensing policy to wider macroeconomic priorities. Consider the 'One Hawker One Licence' policy introduced in 1973. Under the policy, licences were only granted to hawkers who demonstrated a social need or limited upskilling potential — often categorised as those over 40 years old. The Department actively disincentivised entry into the trade and redirected potential hawkers into other priority industries whilst retaining hawking as a social need-only vocation. Details on the policy can be found in Section 2.1 of the Hawker Policy Advisory Committee's report (see Table 7.2).

The One Hawker One Licence policy demonstrates a nuanced approach to restricting hawker supply. Section 2.1.iii of the policy indicates that

Table 7.2.   Policy Excerpts from Section 2.1 of the Hawker Policy Advisory Committee

Section	Policy
2.1.ii	Licences are only issued to Singapore citizens and non-citizens who have been granted permanent residence and have citizen dependents.
2.1.iii	Licences will also be issued to those who are social welfare cases, the physically handicapped and the unemployed who are above 40 years old.
2.1.iv	Applicants under 40 years will not be considered, but will be referred to the Ministry of Labour who have agreed to accord them priority consideration for alternative employment.
2.1.v	No licence will be issued to those engaged in other gainful occupations or business or have other means of income, e.g., shopowners. However, pasar malam hawkers may be shopkeepers.
2.1.vi	Each hawker will be limited to one licence per session except for pasar malam hawkers.

Source: Ministry of Environment/Hawkers Department (HD), 'Hawker Policy Advisory Committee', 1974, 5–6.

licences would only be issued insofar as the recipients demonstrated socioeconomic need or were above 40 years old, presumably because this implied low upskilling potential or more limited opportunities to transition into other employment. Section 2.1.iv, on the other hand, refers able-bodied hawkers to the Ministry of Labour for alternative employment.[19] The Department prohibited the issuance of licences to individuals who did not demonstrate some form of 'social need' that justified working as a hawker. If an applicant could find other sources of income, they had to. Accordingly, 'economically promising' adults were channelled into government-designated productive industries prioritised as part of the wider economic reform. While redirecting would-be and active hawkers helped to mitigate the labour crunch, the policy was also advantageous for hawkers. In Singapore's war- and post-war years, many initially turned to hawking due to a lack of full-time employment options. However, as Singapore's economy restarted itself in the late 1960s and through the 1970s, funnelling hawkers into better-paying industries would have been well-received by hawkers themselves.

A second example was the administration's sensitive approach to enforcing licensing and relocation. Despite having a powerful state apparatus, policy design required finesse given the sensitivities surrounding the hawker problem. Regulations were calibrated with hawkers' own concerns in mind, which mitigated the potential negative impacts of enforcement and further enabled the successful adoption of new hawker policies. One such example can be seen in the hardship policy, found in Section 2.1.iii of the One Hawker One Licence policy (see Table 7.2), which clarified what constituted a 'social need' when considering exceptional cases. According to Goh Chin Tong, the former head of the Department, those who qualified for the hardship policy included individuals who were: (1) receiving state financial aid; (2) physically handicapped; (3) more than 40 years old and unemployed; and/or (4) supporting a family. These 'needy' individuals who met these criteria were given exceptional consideration for a hawker licence. Successful candidates were allocated vacant low-rent stalls in hawker centres.[20] The hardship policy gave the administration operational wiggle room with regards to enforcing the One Hawker One Licence policy and general hawker licensing. It allowed applicants who might otherwise have been held ineligible to still be gainfully employed, albeit now with the government able to monitor, approve and better regulate labour allocation within the economy.

A final example of the government's sensitive approach to policy can be observed from the operational factors they considered when forcibly relocating hawkers into hawker centres. A key consideration mentioned by Goh was the hawkers' 'catchment area' of customers.[21] Hawkers were mostly relocated to a hawker centre close to their original catchment area, either within walking distance or serviceable by a short bus trip, mitigating the potential loss of customers caused by the relocation. This served to cushion the possible impacts of a forced move, encouraging cooperation and avoiding political blowback. To further incentivise relocation, hawkers were given subsidised rates for stall rentals. In the late 1970s, subsidised rates for stalls in hawker centres were around $120–$300 a month, while stalls within privately-owned coffeeshops could go up to the thousands. This subsidised rate was gradually phased out through the natural attrition of hawkers (e.g., illness, death, retirement), with rates eventually replaced by a tender system and subsidies issued on a need-only basis (more in Chapter 9).

This nuanced approach was a significant departure from that of the colonial era. Compared to the top-down colonial rule, where policies were designed and implemented without much buy-in from the public or hawkers, the PAP's new policies were more sensitive and calibrated. Colonial hawker policy was mainly a knee-jerk reaction to hawker overpopulation, which failed to take into account long-term considerations like unemployment, productivity or the potential loss of business to hawkers. Further, hawker shelters were only built in areas that were already congested, where enforcement happened sporadically or did not happen at all.

The 1973 'Extensive Hawker Control Programme'

Despite the rapidly growing economy, the Department's reorganisation and growth from 1965 to 1972, years of licensing success and the introduction of hawker centres, unlicensed hawker numbers were still relatively high. As of late 1972, hawker numbers hovered around 30,000, constituting a hawker population density of 1.44%.[22] This was not satisfactory to the government, prompting then-Permanent Secretary E. Ittogi of the Ministry of Environment to issue an 18-month deadline for the Department to remove all illegal hawkers from the streets. This programme marked the beginning of efforts to conclusively tackle the hawker issue in Singapore.

The agenda was put into practice in July 1973, when the Ministry of Environment launched an 'extensive hawker control programme' in hopes of bringing all unlicensed hawkers under control within six months.[23] Displaced hawkers were to be relocated into nearby hawker centres or *pasar malams* adjacent to new public housing estates and close to their original locations. Ittogi also set up a Department Special Squad, a temporary auxiliary squad of enforcement officers, to boost the Department's strength. While exact data on the size of the special squad is not publicly available, it is likely that its manpower needs were filled through daily-rated employees, who formed approximately half of the Department in 1973.[24] With daily-rated employees, its enforcement capabilities effectively doubled, with 172 full-time officers and an estimated 170 daily-rated officers under the special squad, bringing enforcement capabilities to a total of 342 enforcement officers in 1973.

The Department's extensive hawker programme was the concluding complex operation that succeeded in eliminating illegal hawking from Singapore's streets. It was coordinated via an operations room set up in the Princess House Annexe, and officers were supported by a fleet of 21 vans equipped with radiotelephone sets. Across a six-month period, the Department removed a total of 296 lorries' worth of equipment and material, issued 1,810 warnings and 13,875 tickets amounting to $26,130 worth of goods, and oversaw 13,979 disputes that were dealt with in the courts.[25] By the end of the programme, a total of 10,351 new licences had been issued, bringing the population of licensed hawkers to an acceptable low of 22,335 (a 1.02% hawker population density), the lowest it has ever been since Phase 1.[26] The Department declared the programme a success, with the "task of bringing the unlicensed hawker situation in the Republic under control…successfully accomplished"[27] and marking the end of the hawker reform.

Following the conclusion of the 1973 operation, the government's focus shifted to building enough hawker centres to house newly licensed hawkers and creating employment to complement the One Hawker One Licence policy. A total of 54 additional hawker centres were constructed between 1974 and 1979, representing an average construction rate of nine hawker centres a year.[28] An estimated 18,000 hawkers were successfully relocated between 1971 to 1986.[29] Meanwhile, the government continued nudging hawkers into other productive industry. Minutes from a 1976 inter-ministry seminar on hawker policy indicate that the prohibitive policies of the hawker reform had successfully curbed the proliferation of new hawkers.[30] It also projected an increase in demand for hawker food, driven by the continued expansion of the industrial programme and the corresponding growth in the working population. Figure 7.6 substantiates this, compiling the demographic change among hawkers by age group from 1976 to 1979, where a large portion of the decrease in hawker numbers came from those age 40 and below. The outlier of this trend, the under-16 age group, is perhaps negligible, given that the group had only 28 hawkers, or 0.17% of all recorded hawkers in January 1979, an increase that may be attributable to 'social need' circumstances. Although we do not have demographic data of hawkers prior to the hawker clean-up, we see how the One Hawker One Licence policy successfully shifted the demographic makeup of the hawking industry, based on the decision to restrict the granting of licences.

Figure 7.6.   Average Age of Hawkers (1976 to 1979)

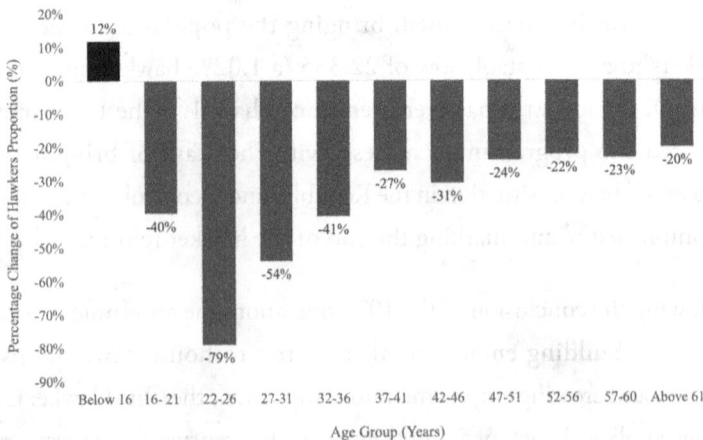

Source: Ryan Kueh 2024. Compiled using data from Ministry of Environment/Hawkers Department (HD) Statistics on Hawker Licences 1979.

Figure 7.7.   Number of Hawkers with Population (1966 to 1978)

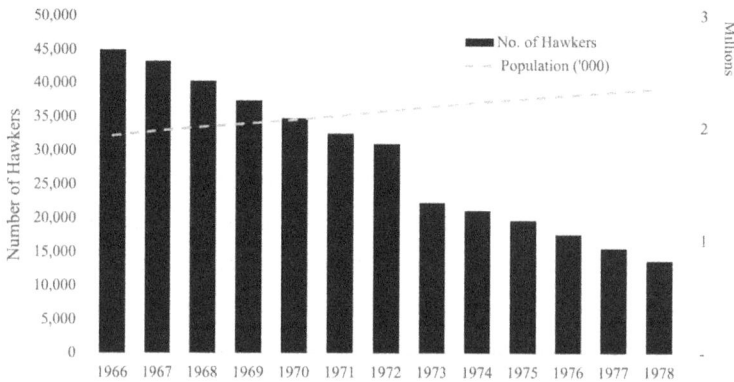

Source: Ryan Kueh 2024. Compiled from Ministry of Environment/Hawkers Department (HD) Annual Report 1971–1973, 11; Ministry of Environment/Hawkers Department (HD) Statistics on Hawker Licences 1979, 2–3, 46, 53, 63, 120; World Bank, retrieved 2023.

Altogether, the PAP's policies were effective at reducing the hawker population. Over a nearly 15-year period, hawker numbers declined by 69%, falling from 45,000 in 1966 (2.33% of the population; see Figure 7.7) to 13,763 in 1978 (0.58% of the population).

Conclusion

The PAP carried out its hawker reform through the four bureaucratic instruments of hawker-related legislation, capacity-building of the Department's operational capabilities, the rapid implementation of hawker centres and calibrated enforcement policies. These instruments were not entirely novel, but the scale and depth at which they were carried out were. First, legislative developments such as the EPHA and SFA introduced new social and hygiene standards that governed hawker operations and laid the legal groundwork necessary for effective policy enforcement. Second, over the late 1960s to the early 1970s, the Department grew its enforcement and planning capabilities to enable effective licensing and enforcement of hawker-specific policies. Within eight years, the Department had nearly doubled in size, and a restructuring further enhanced its capabilities. Third, hawker centres (with added features that distinguished them from their colonial shelter predecessors) and night markets were built at speed to house newly-licensed hawkers and impose a permanence and operational and spatial discipline to the sector. To achieve this, the Department worked with other government and private agencies throughout the construction process. Fourth, hawker policies were sensitive and well-designed. Policies such as One Hawker One Licence scheme were calibrated to align with larger economic considerations, redirecting current and prospective hawkers into priority sectors whilst simultaneously retaining hawking as a social need-only trade. These policies displayed sensitivity towards hawkers' needs and concerns, as can be seen by the Department's 'hardship policy' exception for licensing and relocating hawkers within their 'catchment areas' to minimise loss of business. Finally in 1973, a final 'extensive hawker control programme' was carried out, bringing the population down to a level the government deemed acceptable.

Hawker reform was thus a sophisticated multi-year plan that spanned many moving parts and benefited from good policy design. From the PAP's foresight in recognising the political and economic ramifications of the 'hawker problem', to executing the legislative and organisational changes needed to ramp up licensing and build hawker centres, hawker reform was a whole-of-government initiative that required simultaneous planning, coordination and enforcement. This impressive feat speaks to the growth of state strength under the PAP, for no single instrument could have adequately addressed illegal hawking. Together, however, the orchestra of developments allowed for a successful resolution of the hawker problem in Singapore and a permanent reform of the hawking industry.

This concludes the historical section of this book. Chapters 8 and 9 will focus on a discussion of contemporary hawking, examining how hawking's forms and functions have evolved in the decades since the hawker reform.

Chapter 8
Hawker Centres as Aspired Multiculturalism

🍴

Lily Kong describes the hawker centre as a microcosm of Singapore society: "convenient places serving up affordable food for executives with demanding schedules and families with busy routines; community places where neighbours meet; and casual places where all social types gather — CEO and office cleaner, grandpa and junior, Chinese, Malay, Indian and others."[1] Her description sums up how most Singaporeans today conceive of hawker culture — an 'equalised' dining experience that cuts across class and race, where people from various backgrounds can gather around affordable and convenient food. This conception of hawking, however, is a relatively recent phenomenon, and is rooted in the introduction of hawker centres in the early 1970s.

Prior to that, hawking could be thought of as organic and itinerant, with hawkers sprawling around the streets and clustering by ethnicity and dialect groups. It was a trade predominantly practised by Chinese and Indian immigrants. The introduction of hawker centres, however, changed the culture of consumption and fundamentally altered the way hawking was conducted. Now, hawking is sanitised and controlled, with hawkers of all ethnicities spread out across various public housing estates. This shift in *modus operandi* has also brought about a secondary effect, with hawker centres emerging as a social policy instrument. As an integral public utility for Singaporeans, it is an extension of, and a conduit for, the government's wider social engineering policies such as the Ethnic Integration Policy (EIP), helping to foster and reproduce multicultural relations and advancing Singapore's multicultural agenda.

What about the hawker centre led to such drastic shifts in hawking practices? What other influence do hawker centres have on society? How does the hawker centre interact with other government policies in daily life? This chapter seeks to discuss these questions. To do this, we will first deliberate the ethnic dimensions of hawking in the colonial era, specifically on which ethnic groups dominated the trade and why. Second, we discuss the shifts in Singapore's conception of national identity and social fabric after independence, with a special focus on multiculturalism. Finally, we will touch on how hawker centres are equalising instruments that changed the culture of consumption and the way hawkers operated, ultimately becoming conduits of a wider social engineering policy.

Ethnic Dimensions of Hawking in the Colonial Era

Hawking in pre-independent Singapore was heavily influenced by the migrant Chinese and Indian populations. As explored in Chapter 4, after the establishment of the British colony, waves of migration displaced the native Malay population as the dominant ethnic group. Amongst other sociological changes, this ethnic displacement eventually led to a disproportionate number of Indians and Chinese participating in the hawker trade. In the 1950s, there was a noticeable overrepresentation of Chinese and Indian hawkers compared to Malay. Surveys from the *Report of the Hawkers Inquiry Commission (1950)* show that Chinese hawkers accounted for 84% of all hawkers, with Indian hawkers the second-largest group at 14% (see Table 8.1 and Figure 8.1). Conversely, Malays only comprised 2% of hawkers. The domination of the trade by Chinese and Indian hawkers becomes all the more evident when comparing the ethnic breakdown of hawkers to that of the population. Proportionally, Indians were most likely to undertake hawking, although Chinese hawkers comprised the largest gross ethnic population. This objective dominance of Chinese hawkers was so pronounced that the 1950 Commission even labelled hawking as a 'Chinese problem', attributing it to Chinese individualism and "the desire of the ordinary man to work on his own account and be his own master".[2]

Table 8.1.   Breakdown of Population and Hawkers by 'Race' (1950)

Race	Total Population	Racial Breakdown of Population (%)	Hawkers by Race (%)	Propensity of the Race to Undertake Hawking (Hawkers by Racial Breakdown of Population)
Chinese	789,160	77.72	84	1.08
Malay	123,624	12.17	2	0.16
Indians	72,467	7.14	14	1.96
Others	30,202	N/A	N/A	N/A

Note: There are no numbers for "Others" as the 1950 Commission did not record hawkers of other ethnicities categorised as "Others".

Source: Ryan Kueh 2024. Compiled from 1950 Hawkers Inquiry Commission, 69; 1951 Straits Settlement Annual Report, 73.

Figure 8.1.   Percentage Distribution of Hawkers by 'Race', 1950

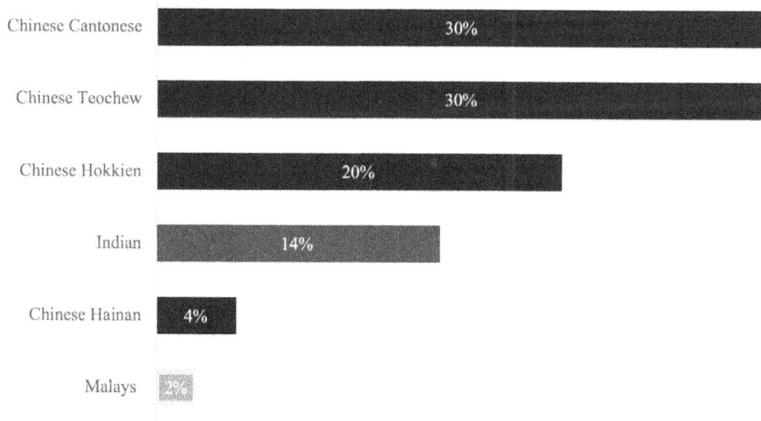

Source: Ryan Kueh 2024. Compiled from Hawkers Inquiry Commission 1950, 69.

Syed Hussein Alatas' post-colonial critique, *The Myth of the Lazy Native*, may provide us with insights as to why hawking was predominantly an immigrant Chinese and Indian endeavour. In his seminal work, Alatas challenges the colonial stereotype of natives as lazy, or the "indolent native",[3] a trope used to describe the Southeast Asian ethnic groups of various colonised states, including the Malays, Javanese and Filipinos. British colonial authorities frequently perpetuated this stereotype. Frank Swettenham, a British man living in Malaya in 1874, described Malays in the following terms: "[having an] absence of servility, which is unusual in the East... The leading characteristic of the Malay of every class is a disinclination to work." [4] Alatas argues that this image of indolence was relative to the other immigrant ethnicities (Chinese, Indians, Europeans), shaped by the unwillingness of the natives (Malays) to engage in colonial capitalism. The Malays had limited functional contact with the European colonisers and did not function in the total life pattern of colonial capitalism. [5]

Native Malays typically received traditional education and participated in family-run agricultural and subsistence activities, which included rice cultivation, fishing, tending to farm animals and collecting jungle produce. This gave them the ability to survive independently without relying on wage labour. As such, they had little necessity and experience in serving the Europeans, such as by working in bars, hotels and retail shops, and did not play a significant role in the network of European administration, education or otherwise. This led to them being perceived as indolent due to their "unwillingness to become a tool in the production system of colonial capitalism." [6]

This image of the lazy native can be contrasted with that of Chinese and Indian subjects, who were seen as more cooperative and industrious. As immigrants, Chinese and Indian labourers did not have the same set of entrenched subsistence resources — such as family, housing, subsistence agriculture — as the Malays, and surviving in Singapore without participating in colonial labour was nearly impossible. Given their low skills and education, many of these immigrants provided the lowest tiers of labour needed to sustain the colonial economy, and were often employed in mining and estate work such as rubber or cane planting. This gave them more opportunities to interact with the British through administration or direct servitude, contributing to the colonial perception of Chinese and Indian immigrants as industrious and the Malay natives as lazy.

Following Alatas, we can better understand how economic, social and political circumstances served to make hawking a primarily Chinese and Indian phenomenon. There were strong incentives for immigrants to engage in hawking, an easy vocation to take up given its better earning potential and low barriers to entry. For the unemployed, selling home-cooked dishes or snacks on the streets was an easy way to supplement an income. Further, without subsistence networks and with little time to cook and prepare meals, Chinese and Indian immigrants were also much more likely to consume food externally, driving up demand for hawker food. On the other hand, Malays, as natives, had established subsistence networks that allowed them to meet their basic needs without relying on wage labour. Food and sustenance needs could be met through agriculture, fishing or alternative localised means with the help of family members.

Changes in Social Circumstances after Independence

Singapore's social fabric and conception of national identity changed drastically after its separation from Malaysia in 1965. As an 'accidental nation' and the only Chinese-dominated polity in Southeast Asia, surrounded by countries that championed ethnic-based politics, its founding generation of leaders made the construction of a new national identity a priority. The result was Singapore declaring itself a constitutional multicultural state.[7] Politically, enshrining multiculturalism distanced Singapore from its neighbours and ensured equal constitutional rights for all citizens irrespective of 'race'. The new ethos prioritised a 'Singaporean' national identity over others, bounded by a philosophy that the public or collective interest superseded individual identities.

To do this, the government replaced the notion of individual ethnic identity with a nationalist self-definition of 'race', or what sociologist

Chua Beng Huat calls the *hyphenated citizen*, meaning that one was 'Singaporean' first and one's 'race' second. 'Singaporean' identity markers were bounded by the idea that "success came on the basis of merit rather than racial, ethnic, religious, or cultural favouritism".[8] One's 'Singaporean-ess' took precedence, and notions of belonging to an ethnic group were relegated to a supporting role in identity construction. Such racialisation severed immigrant ties to one's 'ancestral land' for a new definition of being Singaporean, where the plethora of ethnic and dialect groups (e.g., Tamil Nadu, Malayalam, Orang Laut, Teochew, Hokkien) were simplified into four major race groups of Chinese, Malay, Indian and Others (CMIO).[9] 'Race' became an umbrella term that consolidated the multiplicity of regional cultures under one's ethnicity, a nationalistic concept that constructed new identity markers for Singaporeans.[10] For example, the Chinese were supposed to espouse Confucian values, the Malays were supposed to follow Islamic principles and the Indians to observe the various South Asian religions, such as Hinduism and Sikhism. This self-definition of race became a tool for governance and 'aspired multiculturalism', requiring the "state to set itself structurally above race, as the neutral umpire that oversees and maintains racial peace and racial equality".[11]

Racially neutral, collectively pragmatic policies were also introduced to further the goal of entrenching multiculturalism. An example is the 1966 bilingual education policy, which mandated English as the *lingua franca* and a 'neutral' language meant to unite the different races together. Within the Chinese and Indian races, the government further discouraged the use of dialects (e.g., Hokkien, Teochew, Malayalam) and promoted a standardised 'mother tongue'. State-mandated 'mother tongues' (e.g., Mandarin, Tamil, Malay) were now taught in schools as a second language.[12] This 'racially neutral' policy allowed the state to prioritise its interests above that of individual racial groups, entrenching its push for a national identity.[13] In other words, the PAP government stripped citizens of their previous notions of identity, an ostensibly equalising process, before building them back into newly racialised, multicultural Singaporeans.

This *modus operandi* also manifested through the hawker reform. For hawkers, this equalisation happened physically, where the forced relocation of hawkers into hawker centres fundamentally changed how hawkers operated. Within a short period, hawking changed from a predominantly privatised and *laissez-faire* trade to a heavily regulated, standardised environment. This move reduced the hawker's sphere of control, with many operational considerations such as seating, cleaning and touting now reclaimed by the government, requiring hawkers to renegotiate their "emotional economies of identity, agency and autonomy."[14] Two effects of this are worth further discussion. First, how did the hawker centre revolutionise hawking as a trade? Second, how did the hawker centre become a node for multicultural reproduction?

Equalisation of Hawking through Hawker Centres

The hawker centre is unique as an equalising space: a physical manifestation of the state's ethos of putting the collective interest first, championing a pragmatic and neutral approach to public utilities in Singapore. This began with the rapid introduction and relocation of hawkers into hawker centres during the 1970s, with the hawker centre introducing physical and behavioural standardisation into the hawking trade. This affected hawkers and consumers alike as both groups had to accommodate to the new government-mandated *modus operandi*.

Before, hawking was organic and itinerant. Consumption of hawker food typically occurred in relatively privatised settings, where hawkers would provide their own dining utilities such as tables and chairs. This encouraged a territorial attitude towards the use of space, with disputes sometimes emerging between hawkers as areas near specific stalls were considered to be 'owned' by the respective hawkers and patrons could only occupy those tables if they purchased food from the corresponding stall. This practice is still common in many street food hubs like those in Bangkok, Penang and Malacca. Within this 'old' hawker culture, hawkers did as they wished and governments would often react to their spontaneity.

The relocation of hawkers into hawker centres drastically changed the way hawkers operated. It forced a departure from the *laissez-faire* style of serving street food, with the government reclaiming a substantial portion of control from hawkers. Asaduz Zaman, the architect who oversaw the development of early hawker centres such as Chinatown Complex Market and Food Centre and Geylang Serai Market and Food Centre in the 1970s, recounted the emphasis on fixed utilities such as public tables and chairs in the design.[15] Planners aimed to shift the control of dining spaces from hawkers to the public (government), 'deterritorialising' hawker spaces and compelling hawkers and consumers to adapt to fixed environments. Operational infrastructure was now to be provided by the government, with hawkers' responsibilities and scope of operations limited to their assigned stall space. By consolidating hawkers within a neutral building, hawkers could no longer lay claim to any 'public space' for their exclusive use. These changes brought order to the trade and fostered a more relaxed and customer-friendly hawker culture, prioritising the public's experience over the hawker's right to operate freely. The overarching objective was to achieve "a balance of 'traditional' eating, reminiscent of its former charming disorder with orderly environments... the search for gastronomical pleasure in company with control of risk."[16] In other words, the government 'nationalised' the hawking trade through hawker centres, where regardless of race or ethnicity, the collective interest now came first. This transition from an unrestricted concept of consumption to a structured one represented a significant change for hawkers (and consumers). Within the hawker centre, every hawker is now subject to the same mores, laws and ancillaries that govern the space. There are no pockets of privilege or exclusivity.

Equalisation of Consumers within Hawker Centres

A related significance of hawker centres is their role in facilitating 'equalising' social engineering policies. Given their prevalence and status as racially neutral spaces, hawker centres have become curated 'third places' — social hubs where people gather outside the confines of their homes ('first place') or workplaces ('second place').[17] 'Third places' organically facilitate and reproduce interpersonal relations, creating a "social of interrelatedness, multiple practices, and negotiation with diverse other people and communities."[18] In contrast to other 'third spaces' such as shopping malls, hawker centres are curated to serve the dietary needs of the multicultural composition of the public housing estates surrounding it. This allows hawker centres to have an important role in shaping everyday notions of aspired multiculturalism.

To best understand why hawker centres are nodes of aspired multiculturalism, we must first understand the central utility of the hawker centre. At their core, hawker centres are meant to agglomerate hawkers who provide food to the public estates surrounding them. Then-Minister for the Environment and Water Resources, Masagos Zulkifli, described hawker centres as "community dining rooms".[19] Food offerings must meet the dietary needs of the estate — a multicultural customer base with varying dietary restrictions, as the composition of residents is itself socially engineered.

Here we must briefly turn to the Ethnic Integration Policy (EIP), the PAP's flagship policy aimed at enmeshing multiculturalism in Singapore's social fabric. Introduced in 1989, the EIP was designed to tackle the ethnic enclaves of the colonial era and foster integration by using racial quotas to ensure diversity in public housing. It aims to "preserve Singapore's multi-cultural identity and promote racial integration and harmony"[20] and create "opportunities for social mixing among Singaporeans of different races."[21] This is achieved by using racial quotas to ensure that the residential demographic of every public housing estate reflects Singapore's overall racial distribution, which is roughly 75% Chinese, 15% Malay, 8% Indian and 2% Others. With over 80% of Singaporeans living in public housing, the EIP exerts considerable influence on the social dynamics of shared public spaces, including hawker centres. Sociologist Robbie Goh suggests that the effect of racial social engineering within public housing extends to ancillary social spaces, including "public areas and amenities — hawker centres, playgrounds, transportation networks and hubs, connecting corridors, parks, shopping centres, and so on — which collectively make up the bulk of public housing estates".[22] In other words, due to the pre-established diversity quota in each public housing estate, estates contain residents from all of Singapore's major racial groups, with hawker centres thus needing to serve their various dietary needs and preferences.

To ensure these are met, the government has established culinary quotas within the hawker centres themselves. The National Environment Agency, the government agency that is responsible for hawker policy, categorises cooked food stalls into five mutually exclusive categories (see Table 8.2). As seen from the table, hawker tenders are grouped based on the types of food being sold.

Table 8.2.   A Guide to Articles of Sale (Cooked Food Stall)

Articles of Sale	Remarks
Cooked Food (Halal)	Sale of cooked food (halal) only. Sale of non-halal food is not allowed.
Cooked Food (Indian Cuisine)	Sale of cooked food (Indian cuisine) only. Sale of non-Indian food is not allowed.
Cooked Food	Sale of any type of cooked food and hot and cold desserts.
Drinks	Sale of hot and cold drinks which include package/bottled/dispenser drinks, small food items like cakes and buns, or sale of other cold drinks such as soya bean drinks, grass jelly drinks, sugar-cane juice.
Cut-Fruits	Sale of all types of fruits in 'cut' form.

Source: National Environment Agency 2023.

A parliamentary exchange in 2011 demonstrates this intent fully:

> *"**Mr Ang Hin Kee** asked the Minister for the Environment and Water Resources whether there is a minimum quota for food stalls selling halal food in hawker centres and, if not, what measures will the Ministry consider to ensure that this need is addressed."*

> *"**Mr Sitoh Yih Pin** asked the Minister for the Environment and Water Resources what initiatives can be taken to facilitate the operation of adequate Indian and Muslim food stalls in hawker centres."*

> *"**Dr Vivian Balakrishnan:** My Ministry acknowledges that there are currently some hawker centres where patrons do not have a choice of halal or Indian food stalls. This is due to the unavailability of vacant stalls or lack of interest from food operators when stalls become vacant.*

> *"To ensure that our hawker centres provide a mix of stalls to serve the different communities, there is a desired quota of 10% for halal food stalls. To achieve this, priority is given by only allowing halal food operators to bid in the first two rounds of tender if the quota is not met. Currently, 86% of hawker centres have at least one halal food stall.*

> *"There is currently no quota for Indian or other types of food stalls. My Ministry is reviewing the current policy on food mix in our hawker centres to improve the situation."*[23]

Whilst it is not known whether the National Environment Agency explicitly limits hawker tender bids or stalls based on ethnicity, the current policy aims to ensure that hawker centres cater to the culinary needs and preferences of all races and religions, fostering an inclusive dining experience. For example, only Muslim hawkers can attain halal certification and provide halal food. However, regardless of whether they are a Malay Muslim or Indian Muslim, the halal food they sell would be suitable for the Muslim community. As such, the categories for hawker stalls concomitantly influence the racial composition of the hawkers operating in hawker centres, resulting in a dining environment that mirrors the multicultural, albeit predominantly Chinese, fabric of the public estates they serve. Comparing this to the historical antipode of ethnic and dialect enclaving, where citizens could only find certain types of food in specific areas, one can now find all types of hawker food side by side within the hawker centre.

This leads to the second point: Hawker centres are neutral conduits in the middle of an engineered environment, thereby facilitating opportunities for multicultural interactions. As 'curated third spaces', hawker centres reduce impediments to members of different races and cultures eating together by aggregating all sorts of ethnic foods and dietary restrictions into one centralised location, providing opportunities for racial intermingling. Malay, Indian and Chinese neighbours can each buy and consume one's ethnic food at the same public table; small interactions can lead to larger ones, creating opportunities for communal acts to build. These interactions take place whilst diners maintain a keen awareness of their own racial identity, with the sharing of food and experiences further redefining the Singaporean's identity given the uniqueness of the interaction of space, food and people.[24] Speaking on the effects of the EIP on kindergartens, then-Senior Minister Tharman Shanmugaratnam described it in the following terms: "[t]he kids go to the same kindergarten, the kids go to the same primary school...where they live, and they grow up together."[25] A similar effect can be seen in hawker centres, a curated space where Singaporeans live, eat and socialise with one another.

Conclusion

The hawker centre permanently changed the way hawking was conducted. Previously, hawking was privately driven and carried out in a largely organic fashion, with itinerant and pushcart hawkers flanking busy streets. It was a trade that was dominated by Chinese and Indian immigrants, who, given their constant need for employment and low wages, had a natural incentive to engage in hawking. Without the same entrenched subsistence networks as the Malays, Chinese and Indian immigrants likely also had greater demand for convenient and cooked food.

This changed after the hawker reform, with hawker centres bringing order, hygiene and racial equalisation to the trade, fundamentally changing the culture of consumption and the way hawking operated. Both consumers and hawkers were subjected to this new order, informed by the PAP government's larger ethos of prioritising collective interests — in particular the formation of a new national identity centred on multiculturalism — ahead of the individual. Given the hawker centre's core utility of serving racially curated public housing estates, hawker centres further became a key conduit for larger social engineering policies such as the EIP to manifest by catering to the different dietary needs of Singapore's major races and facilitating cross-cultural interaction. Ultimately, the hawker centre is a cosmopolitan space that is designed to accommodate cultural differences, allowing individuals from various backgrounds to 'break bread' with one another in a neutral and non-threatening space, facilitating Singapore's desire for a robust, multicultural social fabric.

Chapter 9
Evolving Forms and Functions
of Hawking
🍽

Hawking has been an integral part of life in Singapore for centuries, ensuring affordable, convenient access to food since at least the Temasik era. After independence, the widespread social and economic reforms of the 1970s have transformed Singapore into one of the most developed and expensive countries in the world. Likewise, the hawking industry has undergone similarly extensive transformations, with economic development and hawker reform driving changes within the trade. This has resulted in two interesting phenomena. First, despite Singapore being one of the most expensive cities in the world, hawker food is somehow still relatively affordable. What then, has changed to allow the continued affordability and accessibility of hawker food? Second, hawkers have come to serve a new function as stewards of Singapore's culinary heritage. However, as many hawkers age and retire, their culinary traditions are retiring alongside them. What other sociological developments has this development informed?

This chapter seeks to illuminate these evolutions of form and function. To do this, we will first discuss the continued importance of hawking in Singapore, both as a source of affordable food for the masses and other ways in which it is integral to the Singaporean way of life. Next, we will explore two sociocultural evolutions of hawking brought about by economic development. The first is one of form, where we will examine how the nature of access to affordable food in Singapore has evolved. Specifically, we unpack how hawkers continue to provide affordable food in present-day Singapore and what roles the government and hawker centres play in this. The second evolution is one of function, where we discuss how hawkers and the hawking trade have come to play a role as stewards of culinary traditions. This has further resulted in novel trends in response to this disappearing heritage, seen through practices such as the commoditisation of hawker recipes and youths giving up white-collared jobs for a life of hawking.

Affordability and Importance of Hawker Food in Singapore

Despite being routinely ranked as one of most expensive cities in the world,[1] Singapore's 'food programme' is ranked as one of the most affordable. The Economist's Global Food Security Index 2022 — which assesses various food-related factors, including affordability and availability, amongst others — ranks Singapore second in affordability and third in accessibility. How then is Singapore simultaneously expensive and affordable? In this section, we explore two interrelated but separate reasons for hawker food's continued importance, first as a source of affordable food and second as a basic need in Singaporean households.

First, dining out in Singapore is affordable. In 2016 and 2023, researchers from the National University of Singapore (NUS) investigated intra-regional differences in the cost of eating out within Singapore. The reports, aptly titled *The Makan Index* (2016) and *The Makan Index 2.0* (2023) — '*makan*' being Malay for 'to eat' — created an index of prices of food and beverages at hawker centres, coffeeshops and food courts. The 2023 iteration found that the average individual cost of eating out in a hawker centre, food court or coffeeshop for three meals a day, every day for a month, came to $506.70.[2] While not a robust metric of food affordability per se, The Makan Index allows us to construct a hypothetical, if extreme, 'food away from home' (FAFH) spending scenario where an individual or household meets their dietary needs by eating out for all three main meals a day, every day. Individuals would spend about 9.75% of their monthly income on eating out entirely, based on a median income of $5,197 in 2023.[3] Households (defined as partnered parents with two children) would spend roughly 20% of their monthly income, based on a median income of $10,999 in 2022.[4]

Most other developed countries spend around 12% of their total income on food and about a third of that food budget on eating out sporadically. In the European Union, the average percentage of household expenditure on food in 2021 was 14.3%, with Germany and Denmark both at the lower end with 11.8%.[5] Of this, European countries spend 3–5% of their total monthly expenditure, or about a quarter to half of their total food budget on eating out (i.e., FAFH).[6] What is interesting is the vast differences in frequency of eating out, where the majority of Germans (44.83%) only reported eating out once a month,[7] whilst the majority of Danes reported eating out only two to 11 times a year.[8] In the U.S., the share of personal disposable income spent on food is similar; as of 2021, total food expenditure stood at 11.26% of one's income, comprising 5.62% spent on food at home and 5.64% on FAFH.[9] On the whole, Americans dine out more frequently, with 29% claiming to eat out once a week or more, 22% eating out once a month and 18% once every two weeks.[10] In sum, developed countries spend a considerable amount (up to 50%) of their monthly food budget to eat out around once or twice a month.

The takeaways here are twofold. First, people in Western developed countries spend roughly similar proportions of their income on food. Second, they tend to cook their own meals at home, and dining out is a unique or occasional event rather than a realistic and regular method of meeting one's daily dietary needs. Conversely, in Singapore, individuals are able to eat out for every meal whilst spending a similar proportion of their income on food. Taking The Makan Index 2.0's average as an extreme case — where one eats out every day, three meals a day — the hypothetical FAFH spending for an average Singaporean individual, at 9.75% in 2023, is lower than the actual food expenditure in other developed countries (e.g., U.S. at 11.26%). This is not the case for households, with the additional consideration of dependents raising the relative cost of eating out to levels above that in Europe. We must, however, keep in mind that dining out every day is likely not a common practice. Rather, the larger point is that Singaporeans can realistically afford to eat out entirely, a situation that has larger ancillary effects such as ameliorating time poverty (to be discussed in more depth later).

This leads us to our second point, where hawker food is seen as a basic need in Singaporean households. To supplement the case for whether eating out on hawker food is indeed a habitual practice, we draw on the results of the Minimum Income Standard (MIS) study. Summarily, the MIS is a methodology used to determine household budgets required for a basic standard of living in a particular society. It is grounded on consensus-based focus group discussions, allowing the results to reflect the ordinary habits and lived realities of members of the society in question, in this case, Singaporeans. The MIS' salience comes from its function not as a survey of spending habits but rather as an aspirational goal or budget based on empirical inputs. It is a consensual definition of what is required for the minimum dignified standard of living in Singapore, with variations according to the size and makeup of households.

According to MIS surveys conducted in 2019 and 2021, hawker food is an integral line item in the budgets of surveyed Singaporean households.[11] Singaporeans across various demographic backgrounds and socio-economic classes agreed that hawker food is a basic need, with budgets tabulated across both reports identifying it as one of the items taking up the largest proportions of a household or individual's weekly spending. In the 2021 study, for example, partnered parents with two children apportioned $238.40 or 16.12% of their weekly budget for hawker food.[12] This placed hawker food as the second-highest line item on their budget, behind only housing payments. For a single-parent household with one child, hawker food took up 11.02% of their weekly budget, the third-highest line item behind housing payments and tuition fees. Assuming that mortgage payments and school tuition fees are necessary, fixed-sum living costs, hawker food is the most important dietary-related item budgeted for these households. This becomes even more interesting when we consider that the budget for hawker food is higher than that of 'food and non-alcoholic beverages' — assumed to be groceries — meaning that both types of households have a preference for eating out compared to cooking at home.

This preference for hawker food can perhaps be explained by its convenience and accessibility, which help to alleviate time poverty. Time poverty refers to how much free time one has (or does not have) to engage with daily tasks, where individuals in time poverty have less free time. Many households from the middle- and low-income classes are more substantively afflicted with time poverty, making them more likely to eat out as they lack the time to prepare meals at home.[13] As seen from the MIS reports, households with children have a higher budget for eating out than food-based groceries, supporting the notion that households with presumably less time have a larger impetus for dining out. Hawker food is thus a salient social support mechanism that allows Singaporeans to meet daily subsistence needs at a lower monetary and time cost.

Hawker Centres as Instruments of Affordable Food

Despite the rapid changes in its hawking landscape over the last 50 years, including the formalisation of the trade and a shrinking hawker population, Singapore has somehow managed to keep hawker food prices low. As explored in earlier chapters, hawkers have provided the public with affordable meals at least since the Temasik era. Especially during the colonial era, the trade was largely unregulated and informal, with hawker food prices kept low given cheap input costs, a lack of mandatory fees (e.g., rent and licensing fees due to ease of evasion) and a large supply of hawkers. Since the post-independence hawker reform, however, hawking has been politically and economically disincentivised, which permanently reduced the supply of hawkers. As a result, the responsibility for providing affordable food has shifted from market forces to the government, which adopted the utility of hawker food as a consumption-based social support mechanism under its wider governance agendas. To do this, the state has relied on two main policy instruments. The primary one is substantial rental subsidies within hawker centres, whilst the secondary and more recent method is through direct welfare handouts that stimulate demand for hawker food.

Central to the affordability of hawker food in Singapore are the large rental subsidies given to hawkers within hawker centres. As hawker centres are built on nationalised land, the government has the ability to exercise rent control, suppressing a key cost component for hawkers. This can be understood as a form of subsidy or supply-side welfare redistribution with two tiers: 'subsidised' and 'non-subsidised' hawkers. 'Subsidised' hawkers refer to those who were given additional or 'legacy' rent subsidies in the 1970s during the hawker reform, either to incentivise hawker relocation or to hawkers under the hardship scheme (as discussed in Chapter 7). Conversely, 'non-subsidised' hawkers who are not part of this scheme either have a tendered rent, where they rent stalls based on an auctioned price every month, or have an assessed market rent, where they pay a market rent that has been assessed and set by professional valuers, with a renewable tenancy after an initial three-year term. Either way, both groups of hawkers pay below market rates for their stalls, with 'subsidised' hawkers receiving more rent assistance. Rent control substantively defrays costs from hawkers, which incentivises them to provide affordable food. According to a 2014 study on the cost drivers of hawking by the Ministry of Environment and Water Resources, the Ministry of Manpower and the Ministry of Trade and Industry, the hawker population was then about evenly split between subsidised and non-subsidised cooked food hawkers.[14] At the time, the average monthly rent for a subsidised stall was 84% cheaper than a non-subsidised stall, with the average rent for the former around $200 and $1,250 for the latter. For a non-subsidised hawker stall, rent constituted 12% of a hawker's average cost structure, with raw materials the largest component at 59% and manpower costs at 17%. By contrast, the proportion of rent relative to total expenses for subsidised hawkers was much lower, at only 2.5%. The study further found that food prices were least sensitive to rental costs and most sensitive to raw material costs, making rent one of the factors least likely to influence food prices compared with ingredients or manpower. For both subsidised and non-subsidised stalls, a 1% increase in rent only led to a 0.03% increase in consumer food prices, whereas a 1% increase in raw material costs resulted in a 0.56% increase.

The government's ability to maintain such low rental rates for hawker centres is attributable to their nationalisation of land. The government has a monopoly on land usage, allowing them to set prices for the use of public land and thus provide significant back-end rental subsidies for hawkers. This shields hawkers from private-market valuations and reduces rent expenses for hawkers — which would otherwise be substantial — allowing hawkers to benefit from lower overall operating costs and offer affordable food to consumers without severely affecting their profit margins. The government's support further extends to non-financial initiatives as well. For example, upgrading and maintenance of hawker centres is fully funded by the government, with no costs borne by the hawkers themselves.[15] While so-called Repairs and Redecoration (R&R) works take place every five to seven years, hawker rents are not raised nor impacted by the renovation; in fact, hawkers who are unable to operate their stalls due to R&R work may even be given rental remission. This demonstrates the government's willingness to cushion hawkers from financial pressures and ensure they are operating in continuously upgraded hawker centres.

In the last few years, hawkers' cost drivers and their ratio to overall expenses have remained largely the same, due to the government actively introducing more subsidies to support hawkers. An updated study by the Ministry of Environment and Water Resources in 2018 found that the cost drivers for hawkers did not change, with raw materials still constituting the largest cost component for hawkers.[16] Nonetheless, new initiatives were introduced in response to inflation and rising manpower costs. For example, the government announced new productivity measures such as centralised dishwashing and automated tray return systems, with accompanying subsidies ranging from 30% to 70% to directly defray the costs of the centralised dishwashing services.[17] Rental costs have also not substantially changed since the 2014 study and 2018 update, due to multiple rent reliefs which were extended to hawkers from 2020 to 2022 during the Covid-19 pandemic. Senior Minister of State Amy Khor, speaking during a government budget debate in 2023, mentioned that the median monthly rent across non-subsidised cooked food stalls had remained at $1,250 since 2018, with rental costs accounting for approximately 9% of hawkers' operating costs.[18] This proportion is even lower than the figure in the 2014 study, where rent amounted to 12% of hawkers' operating costs. Accounting for inflation, this means that more indirect subsidies have been progressively disbursed through the years by means of rent control between 2014 and 2023.

In contrast, privately-run coffeeshops or food courts often charge significantly higher rents, reaching up to as much as $10,000 per month in 2022.[19] These rates are nearly eight times higher than those for non-subsidised hawker stalls ($1,250 as of 2023) and a staggering 50 times higher than subsidised hawker stalls, assuming subsidised hawker rents have remained unchanged since 2014. The significantly higher rental costs for coffeeshop tenants mean they either have to charge higher prices for similar items or lower their margins to match food prices in hawker centres. This has prompted many coffeeshop tenants to opt out of their rental agreements entirely — understandably so, given the cost challenges of competing with their hawker centre counterparts. At the same time, the exorbitant coffeeshop rents are perhaps a better reflection of the true market-appraised cost of land, demonstrating the extent to which rental costs have been absorbed by the government.

Aside from supply-side subsidies, the government also utilises demand-side levers to keep food affordable in Singapore. In recent years, the government has directly distributed welfare handouts and vouchers that can be used to purchase hawker food. Community Development Council vouchers, first introduced in 2020, were initially designed to "help Singaporean lower-income households defray their cost of living and at the same time, to support hawkers and heartland merchants affected by Covid-19 pandemic."[20] The vouchers come with spending restrictions, and specifically can only be used to buy essential items like food and groceries at local businesses such as heartland enterprises and hawker stalls. Since the initial rollout, the voucher scheme has been extended to all Singaporean households to help offset continual upward pressure on living costs, such as the Covid-19 pandemic, inflation, and an increase in Goods and Services Tax in 2024. By directly issuing welfare handouts and limiting their use to necessities such as hawker food, the impact of the vouchers is twofold: first by defraying subsistence expenses for citizens, and secondly by stimulating demand for hawkers. The use restrictions allow them to work in tandem with other mechanisms keeping food prices low, creating a comprehensive system to keep food continuously affordable for Singaporeans.

We can thus observe that while the role of hawkers as providers of affordable food has remained unchanged, the means through which this is achieved has. Following the hawker reforms of the 1970s, the government has actively intervened to keep hawker food prices low. This has primarily been achieved through extensive rental concessions that shield hawkers from private market forces, where hawkers are charged below market rate for their leases. The secondary, more recent way is through the issuance of welfare vouchers to defray the cost of necessities, limiting their use to items and services such as hawker food and groceries. Through a combination of demand and supply side subsidies, the government has consistently worked to keep hawker costs down, ensuring the collective affordability of food for the masses and financial sustainability for hawkers.

The Evolution of the Hawking Vocation

In modern times, hawkers have taken on a new role: that of cultural stewards. The success of Singapore's economic reforms of the 1970s, along with the government's moves to disincentivise people from joining the hawker trade, brought about long-term risks for the sector. As many lifetime hawkers begin to retire, much of their traditional knowledge are at risk of disappearing alongside them. To this end, hawkers have come to be seen as artisans, stewards of the culinary heritage and traditions of 'old Singapore'. This phenomenon has manifested in two unique ways: first, the commodification of hawking recipes; and second, a shift in people's reasons for entering the trade.

To begin with, we can observe a rise in the commodification of hawker recipes, with some hawkers managing to sell their traditional recipes, handed down through generations, for exorbitant amounts of money. In 2014, Kay Lee Roast Meat was sold for $4 million to the Aztech Group, a Singaporean conglomerate.[21] The deal was initiated by the CEO of the Aztech Group, a long-time patron of the brand. Speaking about the deal, Jeremy Mun, son of the CEO of the Aztech Group, shared that the acquisition was "not about making money, it's about preserving a heritage brand because a lot of good food has disappeared."[22] To buy over Kay Lee, Aztech had to fend off 70 other offers and ended up paying $500,000 more than the initial asking price, and the shop now operates as a subsidiary of the Aztech Group. (It is worth noting that the final $4 million fee included the shopfront housing the stall, which makes it hard to discern the true monetary valuation of the brand's heritage and recipe.)

While some hawkers have successfully sold their recipes for huge sums, most others are not as lucky. In an interview with CNA, the national broadcaster, 70-year-old *kway chap* hawker Phua Gek Sia shared that "[t]here's nobody to take over, but it's a pity to close my stall when I have a good customer base. I have been working as a hawker for 40 years, and I'm tired. I want to find someone to invest in my business and sell my recipes".[23] Phua, like many lifelong hawkers from the 1970s and 1980s, is due to retire from the labour-intensive work, having tired of the long hours and low margins.

China Street Fritters, a popular hawker stall at the Maxwell Food Centre, is another example.[24] Owned by Ng Kok Hua, a second-generation hawker, the stall has been selling traditional handmade Hokkien *ngoh hiang* (meat rolls), liver rolls, sausages and other dishes since 1942. However, difficulties from the Covid-19 pandemic, changes in consumer tastes and the general challenges of running a hawker business forced Ng to close the stall after 81 years. Ng had also personally discouraged his children from taking over the business, not wanting them to inherit the back-breaking life of a hawker.

The Ng family initially sought to sell their recipes for $1 million. With no serious takers, they lowered the price by half to $500,000, a 'goodwill sum' he considered to be fair for his family's retirement. Even then, no buyers met the asking price. As it stands, after closing the stall at Maxwell Food Centre in May 2023, Ng re-opened a scaled down version of his shop in August 2023 at a coffeeshop in Telok Blangah.[25]

The stories of Phua, the *kway chap* hawker, and China Street Fritters are perhaps a more realistic portrayal of most retiring hawkers' situations. A lack of willing buyers for their recipes ultimately leaves Singapore with fewer individuals who possess the knowledge and skills to recreate traditional dishes. Younger Singaporeans are also unwilling to inherit their family's businesses, given the hardships associated with hawking and the presence of better job opportunities elsewhere. A recipe or brand buyout on the scale of Kay Lee's is rare: Even if a business has loyal fans, they may lack the funds or not be interested in becoming hawkers themselves. A more likely reason, perhaps, is that most members of the public do not value preserving hawker heritage at the amounts proposed by the hawkers.

The commodification of hawker food, or the heritage it represents, can perhaps be understood as a tension between Singapore's hyper-globalisation and a desire to assert control over the retention of our cultural heritage. This phenomenon is brought about by a sense of 'lostness' or 'pastness', with many feeling that Singapore's hawker heritage is under threat of extinction. Chua Beng Huat's description of Singaporeans' nostalgia for the *kampung* (village in Malay) best elucidates this. Given Singapore's fast-paced modernisation, many ordinary people, especially from older generations, tend to remember *kampung* life fondly. Chua refers to this remembrance as a positive memorialised representation categorised by a "'relaxed' pace of life, communitarian cooperation and happy days despite material privation."[26] Specifically, nostalgia is evoked as people lament the loss of former communities. In an environment of continued stress brought about by Singapore's cosmopolitanism, this nostalgia is a critique of the present and "is an attempt to control one's life rather than have it controlled by the logic of capital."[27]

This *kampung* nostalgia is similar to gastronomic nostalgia, or the familiar emotional and sensorial connection brought about by consuming 'traditional' or 'authentic' foods — such as the kind often provided by hawkers.[28] For many Singaporeans, especially the older generations, eating traditional foods reminds them of the past, when such foods could be bought either from the itinerant hawkers of the late 1960s and 1970s or in early hawker centres and *pasar malams* (night markets).

Hawker recipe deals such as the Kay Lee buyout hint towards a larger angst amongst Singaporeans to preserve culinary heritage through 'modern' but often inadequate means. Here, the commodification of hawker recipes can be interpreted as attempts to remember, reconnect and exert a sense of control over one's heritage, albeit indirectly. I say 'indirectly', as most concerned Singaporeans are either unwilling to become hawkers themselves or do not have direct access to reproducing their culinary heritage (e.g., via family recipes). While the Kay Lee case involved a buyout, other hawker brands have taken to franchising, with popular hawker stalls such as Yew Kee Duck Rice or Jian Bo Shui Kueh experimenting with new business models to ensure the continuity and success of the brand. Through franchising, Singaporeans who have the financial means but lack the traditional knowhow can own a portion of their favourite brand without directly buying over the entire brand or joining the hawker trade themselves.

These methods are, however, unfortunately inadequate as they do not address the root problems facing the declining hawker trade and are inherently unable to replicate the characteristics that make hawker culture unique. For example, recipe buyouts do not counter the substantive problem that the hawker, the original maker of that recipe, with all their culinary know-how and experience, is retiring. Often, cooking, especially Asian cooking, is an art rather than a science, and nuances in flavour and texture cannot be replicated through recipes and standard operating procedures. Even if a buyer acquires a hawker brand's recipe and intellectual property, replicating a dish is difficult without the appropriate training or apprenticeship under that specific hawker. On the business front, models such as franchising are in tension with the entrepreneurial character of hawking itself, with commercial decisions sometimes resulting in physical changes to a dish. For example, many chain fishball noodle stores use factory-made fishballs given how time-consuming and labour-intensive fishballs are to make, but this takes away the taste and textural deviation that can be found amongst different fishball noodle hawkers who hand-make the fishballs to their own recipe. Commercialisation might employ the rhetoric of hawking, but in the process, loses the entrepreneurial and idiosyncratic nature of hawking that characterised the trade before.

A second way we see the elevation of hawkers to modern cultural symbols is through the evolution of people's motivations for undertaking the trade. In recent times, more news have emerged of well-educated, younger Singaporeans giving up white-collar jobs to take over their family's hawker business. One of them is Li Ruifang, a third-generation hawker who runs 545 Whampoa Prawn Noodles.[29] Li, a university graduate, left an international company and joined her parents in the business as she wanted to preserve her family's prawn noodle recipe, a decision that would be counterintuitive to most. To run the stall, Li works longer hours than at her previous job, with 15-hour days beginning at 2:30 AM. Despite this, Li made the conscious decision to prioritise the preservation of her family's heritage over her personal material comforts. Another example is that of Sim Weijie, a 32-year-old teacher-turned-hawker.[30] Sim's parents run Hung Huat Cakes and Pastries, a third-generation hawker stall at Sims Vista Market and Food Centre. Its recipes were passed down from Sim's grandfather, who used to sell traditional pancakes in a pushcart around the Geylang area before handing over his business to Sim's parents. Sim, who also took a pay cut and now works 15-hour days, shared that preserving his heritage was an intangible motivator that justified the sacrifices, as he did not want to let his ageing parents' business retire with them.

These two examples, barring many others, show us that for some, the underlying motivations for joining hawking have fundamentally changed. For many younger hawkers, hawking is no longer a transitory or stop-gap vocation driven by economic necessity. Rather, they are drawn by a desire to become custodians of their heritage, one strong enough to motivate even youths from well-educated backgrounds or well-salaried professions to willingly 'sacrifice' their prior jobs for. The change in motivations to undertake hawking further represents an internalisation of the potential 'loss' of one's heritage. Unlike the instances of commodification, this new generation of hawkers has access to their heritage through their parents. They are directly concerned with the preservation of foodways — dietary habits, food preparation processes, cooking techniques and cooking spaces — that have been passed down through generations, and actively seek to extend this for at least a few years more.

To address the trend of hawkers retiring with their recipes, the Singapore government has developed policies to actively incentivise people to join the profession. These include:

1. the Hawkers Succession Scheme (HSS), which aims to match veteran hawkers who are intending to retire but are unable to find successors amongst their relatives to potential business partners.[31]

2. the Hawkers Development Programme (HDP), which aims to equip current and aspiring hawkers with the relevant skills to run their business.[32]

Summarily, the HSS looks to facilitate the passing down of businesses from veteran hawkers to aspiring novices, whilst the HDP looks to equip hawkers with vital ancillary skills related to running a business. Although these policies are commendable in their intent, they perhaps do not have a substantive impact in solving the problem. Many of these recipes are 'family secrets', and some retiring hawkers would rather retire with the recipes or sell them for the highest possible price than pass these recipes down for the sake of posterity. It is well within these custodians' right to do so, but the hubris of selling a recipe, an intangible piece of heritage, only further perpetuates the larger trend of these traditions dying out. Ultimately, new ways of preserving the hawker trade, from their recipes to their techniques and skills, are required. But an exploration of such solutions, unfortunately, is beyond the scope of this book.

Conclusion

In this chapter, we have discussed the evolving forms and functions of hawking. Despite substantive changes within the hawking industry, the relative affordability of hawker food has remained, given its function as a key social support mechanism in Singapore. The first evolution is thus one of form rather than function: the nature of provision itself has evolved, from a process that was organically driven by the hawkers themselves to one that the government manages through a complex, socially-engineered food programme to ensure the continued affordability of food in hawker centres. One such tool is using rent control to help defray hawkers' operating costs, creating cost savings which they can then pass on to consumers, along with other levers like welfare vouchers to further keep food affordable. The functions of the hawker trade have also evolved, with hawkers now acquiring a perceived role as trustees of Singapore's culinary heritage and traditions beyond just being a source of cheap meals. With many older hawkers entering retirement, the prospect of losing this culinary heritage has triggered varying responses, from the commercialisation of popular stalls to younger, new-generation hawkers stepping up to the plate and taking over their family businesses.

Whether this is sufficient remains to be seen. Ultimately, Singapore's hawker culture is a living testament to the adaptability, innovativeness and durability of the hawking tradition. As repositories of our cultural practices, hawkers continue to reflect our past, current and future national identities, representing not only our roots but also remaining a familiar sight amidst a perpetually changing Singapore.

Chapter 10
Conclusion

From its possible beginnings in around 14th century Temasik, through the British colonial era to modern-day Singapore, hawking is a trade that has endured. At the same time, it has also undergone drastic evolutions in tandem with the nation's ever-changing political and social circumstances. In this book, we have been able to piece together this historical narrative by studying the people and policies that governed hawking in Singapore, organised into four broad phases:

- **Historical Singapore (ninth to 14th century)**: Chapter 3 looked to challenge colonial narratives of history and touched on the possibilities of hawking existing since around ninth and 14th century ancient Singapore, then known as Temasik. We discussed the conditions that would enable a local hawking population, with good evidence to support the notion that conditions in 14th century Singapore were favourable for hawking. Temasik was richly intertwined with the regional economy and routinely hosted foreign visitors, with historical accounts supporting the presence of local markets, currency-denominated trade and regional merchants. Conversely, such conditions did not appear to be present in ninth century Singapore, as it was overshadowed by more prominent ports in the region. However, hawking was likely to exist in these other ports given their relevance in interregional trade.

- **Phase 1 (1819 to 1942)**: Chapter 4 explored Singapore's early colonial era as the Straits Settlement Crown Colony. Large waves of Chinese and Indian immigration displaced the native Malays as the dominant population, with hawking largely undertaken by unskilled and uneducated immigrants looking for alternative employment. Demand for hawker food was high given its convenience and affordability, with labourers and mid-day clerks forming the main customer base. It was in this phase that we saw the advent of the 'hawker problem' — large numbers of unlicensed hawkers that brought about public health and spatial order issues — driven by rapid population growth. This resulted in the first hawker shelters along with legislation initiated by the colonial government, in an attempt to resolve the issue albeit with little effect given weak enforcement capabilities.

- **Phase 2 (1942 to 1965)**: Chapter 5 explored hawking in World War II and post-war Singapore. In Phase 2, issues surrounding hawkers and their challenges mirrored those observed in Phase 1. The hawker population surged during this period, with hawker population density at an all-time high, an issue that further complicated Singapore's economic recovery. The 1951 Report shed light on the personal drivers behind hawking, supporting the notion that poor post-war economic conditions were what pushed people to join the trade. Like Phase 1, enforcement was rhetorical and weak, with the administration unable to substantively address illegal hawking.

- **Phase 3 (1965 to present)**: Chapters 6 and 7 covered hawking in newly independent Singapore, marked by the People's Action Party's (PAP's) ascent to power. This phase saw the most significant developments within both Singapore at large and the hawking industry. Economic reforms fundamentally disincentivised people from undertaking hawking, and hawkers were instead actively diverted into other industries. Wider hawker reforms were enacted through calibrated hawker-specific policies such as new health-related legislation, effective enforcement, long-term planning and sensitive policymaking. The problem of illegal hawkers was 'solved' in 1973 by licensing and relocating hawkers into rapidly built hawker centres.

From its evolution through the different phases, we can observe that hawking is a multifaceted phenomenon. It is a microcosm of the complex interplay between development economics, political legitimacy and social relations. At its core, hawking is an entrepreneurial response to poor macroeconomic circumstances, a 'self-help' mechanism of surviving by selling home-cooked food on the streets. Hawking helped to feed a developing nation, providing cheap and accessible food to the masses. In short, hawking covered the blind spots of an ineffective state. Despite its many uses, however, uncontrolled hawking can lead to several run-off problems, as we observed in Phases 1 and 2.

Singapore's path to resolving the 'hawker problem' was characterised by multiple cycles of failures and learnings. This was successfully resolved in Phase 3, where an interplay of policy, enforcement and urban planning worked together to reform the hawking industry. Instead of taking the usual approach of either prosecution or total eradication, the PAP government adopted an ethos of integration and sought to retain and develop the hawking sector, with proper guardrails to keep it under control. This formalised the industry and incorporated it into the nation's wider economy and society, preserving both the social utility and culinary heritage of the vocation in the process. Of particular salience is the hawker centre, a novel physical manifestation of control that embodies the state's philosophy of putting collective interest first. The hawker centre used infrastructure to change the culture of consumption and redefine social mores, equalising the trade for hawkers and consumers alike.

To our contemporary sensibilities, hawker centres have also become a central tenet of Singaporean identity and politics. Culturally, hawker centres facilitate the 'aspired multiculturalism' integral to Singapore politics. As an important public feature that serves public housing estates — themselves curated for racial diversity — hawker centres are at once both 'third spaces' for people to gather and a vehicle for social engineering. Hawker centres provide opportunities for citizens of different races to come together, facilitating conversations and interactions across cultures and classes. But hawker centres are also a key policy instrument that allows the government to engage in supply-side welfare redistribution by indirectly keeping food prices low. By giving hawkers substantial rental subsidies, the government reduces their operating costs, allowing these cost savings to be passed on to consumers. This keeps food prices low for Singaporeans, so much so that citizens could realistically afford to eat out for every meal. All in all, however, these effects represent but a fraction of the importance of hawking, and more research needs to be done on how the industry intersects with daily life.

As Singapore continues in its attempts to construct a national identity, hawker culture emerges as a 'tangible' avenue forward, an integral scaffold for something uniquely Singaporean. After all, daily chatter about hawker food and hawker culture is endless: where to go for the best dishes, which stalls are closing, how the culture should best be preserved and so on. But hawker culture is so embedded in everyday life that this has also created a paradox: Many do not feel the urgency to uncover its legacy and origins. This has been the driving reason for this book. As more hawkers retire, taking their businesses with them, my hope for this book is to encourage greater attention and academic study of hawking and hawker centres; to show that, more than just a conversation topic, the subject is worthy of intellectual study and discussion. Laments that hawker culture is dying a slow death make it only more important that it should be studied while stewards of this culture are still with us. And amid all the debate over the origins of certain hawker dishes — many of which Singapore may not be able to fully lay claim to — the hawker centre is truly a uniquely Singaporean innovation, one that Singaporeans should be proud of and appreciate in ways beyond just eating out or reading a book.

Endnotes

ﾞｯﾟ

Chapter 1

1. UNESCO, 'Nomination File No. 01568 for Inscription in 2020 on the Representative List of the Intangible Cultural Heritage of Humanity', 19 December 2020, Nomination file No. 01568, https://ich.unesco.org/en/ RL/hawker-culture-in-singapore-community-dining-and-culinary- practices-in-a-multicultural-urban-context-01568.

2. With the 'first space' being home, and the 'second space' being work.

Chapter 2

1. Ray Bromley, 'Street Vending and Public Policy: A Global Review', *International Journal of Sociology and Social Policy* 20, no. 1/2 (1 January 2000): 1–28, https://doi.org/10.1108/01443330010789052; John C. Cross, 'Co-Optation, Competition, and Resistance: State and Street Vendors in Mexico City', *Latin American Perspectives* 25, no. 2 (1998): 41–61; Maureen Hays-Mitchell, 'Streetvending in Peruvian Cities: The Spatio-Temporal Behavior of Ambulantes*', *The Professional Geographer* 46, no. 4 (1994): 425–38, https://doi.org/10.1111/j.0033-0124. 1994.00425.x; Yandi Andri Yatmo, 'Street Vendors as "Out of Place" Urban Elements', *Journal of Urban Design* 13, no. 3 (1 October 2008): 387–402, https://doi.org/10.1080/13574800802320889.

2. Bromley, 'Street Vending and Public Policy'.

3. Kristina Graaff and Noa Ha, eds., *Street Vending in the Neoliberal City: A Global Perspective on the Practices and Policies of a Marginalized Economy*, 1st edition (New York; Oxford: Berghahn Books, 2015), 3.

4. Graaff and Ha, 3.

5. Asef Bayat, *Life as Politics: How Ordinary People Change the Middle East*, 1st edition (Stanford, Calif: Stanford University Press, 2009), 56.

6. Hernando De Soto, *The Other Path: The Invisible Revolution in the Third World*, 1st edition (New York: HarperCollins, 1989); Yatmo, 'Street Vendors

as "Out of Place" Urban Elements'; Bromley, 'Street Vending and Public Policy'.

7. Mario Lubetkin, 'Informal Economy — Street Vending in Asia' (TerraViva, May 2006), 2–3, https://www.ilo.org/wcmsp5/groups/public/---asia/---ro-bangkok/documents/publication/wcms_bk_pb_117_en.pdf.

8. Hays-Mitchell, 'Streetvending in Peruvian Cities'.

9. Lubetkin, 'Informal Economy — Street Vending in Asia', 2.

10. Paras Singh, 'MCD Set to Conduct Census of Street Hawkers Operating in Delhi', Hindustan Times, 21 August 2023, https://www.hindustantimes.com/cities/delhi-news/mcd-to-conduct-fresh-census-of-street-hawkers-and-vendors-in-delhi-project-expected-to-take-six-months-1016926 41479236.html.

11. Rina Chandran, 'Bangkok Street Vendors: From Michelin Star to Fighting Eviction', Reuters, 17 September 2018, sec. Retail, https://www.reuters.com/article/us-thailand-rights-lawmaking-idUSKCN1LX23V.

12. Adolf Alzuphar and Ivy Beach, 'Street Vending Is Legal in Los Angeles after a Decade of Organizing', Waging Nonviolence (blog), 3 January 2019, https://wagingnonviolence.org/2019/01/street-vending-legal-los-angeles-after-decade-organizing/.

Chapter 3

1. National Heritage Board, 'The History and Evolution of Singapore's Hawker Culture', Roots, 15 December 2021, https://www.roots.gov.sg/en/stories-landing/stories/Serving-Up-a-Legacy.

2. Lily Kong, *Singapore Hawker Centres: People, Places, Food* (National Environment Agency, 2007), https://ink.library.smu.edu.sg/soss_research/1867/.

3. John N. Miksic, *Singapore and the Silk Road of the Sea, 1300–1800* (NUS Press, 2013).

4. Miksic, 94.

5. Miksic, 95–98.

6. Miksic, 96.

7. Miksic, 406.

8. John N. Miksic, 'Products of Ancient Singapore', in *Singapore and the Silk Road of the Sea, 1300–1800* (NUS Press, 2013), 287, https://doi.org/10.2307/j.ctv1nthqk.5.

9. Derek Heng, 'Reconstructing Banzu, a Fourteenth-Century Port Settlement in Singapore', *Journal of the Malaysian Branch of the Royal Asiatic Society* 75, no. 1 (282) (2002): 69–90.

10. It is worth noting that Wang Dayuan classifies Banzu and Longyamen as different settlements altogether, with Banzu potentially (incorrectly) identified as Bintam or Batam, although Rockhill himself has identified the potential incoherence within Wang Dayuan's sources. Also, see Rockhill pg 133 footnote 1.

11. W. W. Rockhill, 'Notes on the Relations and Trade of China with the Eastern Archipelago and the Coast of the Indian Ocean during the Fourteenth Century. Part II', *T'oung Pao* 16, no. 1 (1915): 133.

12. Heng, 'Reconstructing Banzu, a Fourteenth-Century Port Settlement in Singapore'.

13. Rockhill, 'Notes on the Relations and Trade of China with the Eastern Archipelago and the Coast of the Indian Ocean during the Fourteenth Century. Part II', 130–33.

14. Rockhill, 112. See footnote 1: This was before the porcelain factories moved to Chu-Chou in the beginning of the Ming Dynasty (A.D. 1368). Chu-Chou here likely refers to the Chu-Chou (simplified Chinese: 处州), which refers to Lishui County (丽水市) in modern times.

15. Miksic, *Singapore and the Silk Road of the Sea, 1300–1800*, 290.

16. R. O. Winstedt, 'Gold Ornaments Dug Up at Fort Canning, Singapore', *Journal of the Malayan Branch of the Royal Asiatic Society* 6, no. 4 (105) (1928): 3.

17. Winstedt, 4.

18. Heng, 'Reconstructing Banzu, a Fourteenth-Century Port Settlement in Singapore'.

19. Miksic, *Singapore and the Silk Road of the Sea, 1300–1800*, 139–41.

20. John N. Miksic, 'Temasik's Partners in Java, Thailand, Vietnam, Sri Lanka, and India', in *Singapore and the Silk Road of the Sea, 1300–1800* (NUS Press, 2013), 354, https://doi.org/10.2307/j.ctv1nthqk.5.

21. John N. Miksic, 'Ancient Singapore, Urbanism, and Commerce', in *Singapore and the Silk Road of the Sea, 1300–1800* (NUS Press, 2013), 437–39, https://doi.org/10.2307/j.ctv1nthqk.5.

22. Miksic, 'Temasik's Partners in Java, Thailand, Vietnam, Sri Lanka, and India', 362.

23. Miksic, 'Products of Ancient Singapore', 287.

24. Stephen A Murphy, 'Asia in the Ninth Century: The Context of the Tang Shipwreck', in *The Tang Shipwreck: Art and Exchange in the 9th Century* (Asian Civilisation Museum, 2017), 14.

25. Alan Chong, 'Introduction', in *The Tang Shipwreck: Art and Exchange in the 9th Century* (Asian Civilisation Museum, 2017), 10.

26. Murphy, 'Asia in the Ninth Century: The Context of the Tang Shipwreck', 12.

27. Michael Flecker, 'The Origin of the Tang Shipwreck', in *The Tang Shipwreck: Art and Exchange in the 9th Century* (Asian Civilisation Museum, 2017), 37.

28. Chong, 'Introduction', 8.

29. Flecker, 'The Origin of the Tang Shipwreck', 34.

30. Murphy, 'Asia in the Ninth Century: The Context of the Tang Shipwreck', 18.

31. Stephen A. Murphy, 'Ports of Call in Ninth-Century Southeast Asia: The Route of the Tang Shipwreck', in *The Tang Shipwreck: Art and Exchange in the 9th Century* (Asian Civilisation Museum, 2017), 242–43.

32. John N. Miksic, 'Sinbad, Shipwrecks, and Singapore', in *The Tang Shipwreck: Art and Exchange in the 9th Century* (Asian Civilisation Museum, 2017), 226–27.

33. Murphy, 'Asia in the Ninth Century: The Context of the Tang Shipwreck', 19.

Chapter 4

1. John Cameron, *Our Tropical Possessions in Malayan India: Being a Descriptive Account of Singapore, Penang, Province Wellesley, and Malacca; Their Peoples, Products, Commerce, and Government* (Smith, Elder and Co, 1865), 65, https://eresources.nlb.gov.sg/printheritage/detail/7658c549-f1c5-47c7-b8b6-831f7eb90c58.aspx.

2. Tai Yong Tan, *The Idea of Singapore: Smallness Unconstrained*, IPS-Nathan Lecture Series (World Scientific, 2019), 86–90, https://doi.org/10.1142/11640; Constance Turnbull, *A History of Modern Singapore, 1819–2005*, 4th ed. (National University of Singapore Press, 2020).

3. Thomas John Newbold, *Political and Statistical Account of the British Settlements in the Straits of Malacca, Viz. Pinang, Malacca, and Singapore: With a History of the Malayan States on the Peninsula of Malacca* (J. Murray, 1839), 307–8, https://eresources.nlb.gov.sg/printheritage/detail/8123f6c8-67a1-48c6-97a6-3357c3bc5966.aspx.

4. Chee Kiong Tong, 'Chinese in Singapore', in *Encyclopedia of Diasporas: Immigrant and Refugee Cultures Around the World*, ed. Melvin Ember, Carol R. Ember, and Ian Skoggard (Springer US, 2005), 723–32, https://doi.org/10.1007/978-0-387-29904-4_75.

5. Arnold Wright, *Twentieth Century Impressions of British Malaya: Its History, People, Commerce, Industries, and Resources* (Lloyd's Greater Britain Publishing Company, limited, 1908), 37, https://digital.library.cornell.edu/catalog/sea233.

6. James F. Warren, *Rickshaw Coolie: A People's History of Singapore, 1880–1940* (NUS Press, 2003), 19.

7. Philip A. Kuhn, *Chinese Among Others: Emigration in Modern Times, State and Society in East Asia* (Rowman & Littlefield Publishers, 2008).

8. C. M. Turnbull, *A History of Singapore, 1819–1988*, 2nd ed. (Oxford University Press, 1989), 96.

9. Brij V. Lal, Peter Reeves, and Rajesh Rai, eds., *The Encyclopedia of the Indian Diaspora* (University of Hawaii Press, 2007), 176–79; Turnbull, *A History of Singapore, 1819–1988*, 96–97.

10. Lal, Reeves, and Rai, *The Encyclopedia of the Indian Diaspora*, 177.

11. Lily Kong, *Singapore Hawker Centres: People, Places, Food* (National Environment Agency, 2007), https://ink.library.smu.edu.sg/soss_research/1867/.

12. Chee Kien Lai, *Early Hawkers in Singapore: 1920s to 1930s* (Focus Publishing, 2020).

13. Ah Eng Lai, 'The Kopitiam in Singapore: An Evolving Story about Cultural Diversity and Cultural Politics', in *Food, Foodways and Foodscapes*, World Scientific Series on Singapore's 50 Years of Nation-Building (World Scientific, 2014), 106, https://doi.org/10.1142/9789814641234_0006.

14. Kiyomi Yamashita, 'The Residential Segregation of Chinese Dialect Groups in Singapore: With Focus on the Period before ca. 1970', *Geographical Review of Japan* 59 (Ser. B), no. 2 (1986): 90.

15. Cornelius-Takahama Vernon, 'Ellenborough Market', SingaporeInfopedia, 2005, https://eresources.nlb.gov.sg/infopedia/articles/SIP_480_2005-01-07.html.

16. National Heritage Board, 'Former Tekka Market', Roots, 23 June 2022, https://www.roots.gov.sg/places/places-landing/Places/landmarks/little-india-heritage-trail-serangoon-in-the-1900s/former-tekka-market.

17. Saw Swee-Hock, 'Population Trends in Singapore, 1819–1967', *Journal of Southeast Asian History* 10, no. 1 (1969): 39.

18. W. Bartley, 'Report of the Committee Appointed to Investigate the Hawker Question in Singapore' (Colonial Secretary Singapore, 4 November 1931), 8.

19. Bartley, 8.

20. Kong, *Singapore Hawker Centres: People, Places, Food.*

21. Bartley, 'Report of the Committee Appointed to Investigate the Hawker Question in Singapore', 8.

22. Tin Seng Lim, 'Hawkers: From Public Nuisance to National Icons', *Biblioasia*, 1 October 2013, https://biblioasia.nlb.gov.sg/vol-9/issue-3/oct-dec-2013/singapore-hawkers-national-icons/.

23. Kong, *Singapore Hawker Centres: People, Places, Food.*

24. Kong; Lai, *Early Hawkers in Singapore: 1920s to 1930s*; Azhar Ghani, 'A Recipe for Success: How Singapore Hawker Centres Came to Be', *IPS Update* Success Matters: How Singapore Hawker Centres Came to Be (May 2011), https://lkyspp.nus.edu.sg/docs/default-source/ips/ag_history-of-hawkers_010511.pdf; Beng Huat Chua, 'Taking the Street Out of Street Food', in *Food, Foodways and Foodscapes*, World Scientific Series on Singapore's 50 Years of Nation-Building (World Scientific, 2014), 23–40, https://doi.org/10.1142/9789814641234_0002.

25. Lai, *Early Hawkers in Singapore: 1920s to 1930s.*

26. Bartley, 'Report of the Committee Appointed to Investigate the Hawker Question in Singapore', 7.

27. Brenda S. A. Yeoh, 'The Control of "Public" Space: Conflicts over the Definition and Use of the Verandah', in *Contesting Space in Colonial Singapore*, Power Relations and the Urban Built Environment (NUS Press, 2003), 262–63, https://doi.org/10.2307/j.ctv1ntj2v.21.

28. Naidu Thulaja, 'Travelling Hawkers', SingaporeInfopedia, 2016, https://eresources.nlb.gov.sg/infopedia/articles/SIP_47_2004-12-27.html.

29. Lim, 'Hawkers'.

30. Yeoh, 'The Control of "Public" Space', 262–66.

31. John Kwok, 'How Singapore's Hawker Culture Started', *TodayOnline*, 10 September 2019, https://www.todayonline.com/commentary/how-singapores-hawker-culture-started.

32. Bartley, 'Report of the Committee Appointed to Investigate the Hawker Question in Singapore', 8.

33. Bartley, 'Report of the Committee Appointed to Investigate the Hawker Question in Singapore'.

34. Bartley, 3.

35. Yeoh, 'The Control of "Public" Space', 255.

36. Yeoh, 262.

37. Straits Settlements Blue Books, 1931, RM: I F/62, Raffles Museum and Library, 204–205, viewed at National Archives of Singapore.

38. Yeoh, 'The Control of "Public" Space', 266.

39. Bartley, 'Report of the Committee Appointed to Investigate the Hawker Question in Singapore', 30–34.

40. Bartley, 117.

41. Ghani, 'A Recipe for Success: How Singapore Hawker Centres Came to Be'.

42. Bartley, 'Report of the Committee Appointed to Investigate the Hawker Question in Singapore', 7.

Chapter 5

1. Geok Boi Lee, 'Wartime Victuals: Surviving the Japanese Occupation', *Biblioasia*, 21 April 2019, https://biblioasia.nlb.gov.sg/vol-15/issue-1/apr-jun-2019/wartime-victuals/.

2. From the oral history interview of Wong Hiong Boon 黄相文 (Accession No. 003526, Track No. 04), Oral History Centre, National Archives of Singapore.

3. From the oral history interview of Lu Yaw (Accession No. 001599, Track No. 07), Oral History Centre, National Archives of Singapore.

4. From the oral history interview of Jean Yip and Dawn Yip (Accession No. 002951, Track No. 01), Oral History Centre, National Archives of Singapore.

5. Hawkers Inquiry Commission, 'Report of the Hawkers Inquiry Commission, 1950' (Colony of Singapore, 30 September 1950), 15, Reference Closed Collection (RCLOS), National Library of Singapore.

6. Statement by Mr. Yong Nyuk Lin, Minister for Health, at the Press Conference Held at the Administrative Headquarters of the Hawkers Department, Junction of Scotts Road with Newton Circus on Wednesday, 9th February, 1966 at 1600 Hours, 09 February 1966, PressR19660209b, Ministry of Culture, 1, viewed at National Archives of Singapore.

7. Hawkers Inquiry Commission, 'Report of the Hawkers Inquiry Commission, 1950', 5.

8. Hawkers Inquiry Commission, 46.

9. Hawkers Inquiry Commission, 46.

10. Hawkers Inquiry Commission, 'Report of the Hawkers Inquiry Commission, 1950'.

11. Hawkers Inquiry Commission, 27.

12. Hawkers Inquiry Commission, 70.

13. 1950 hawker numbers (25,000) × Hawkers who began hawking after the war (50%).

14. Hawkers Inquiry Commission, 'Report of the Hawkers Inquiry Commission, 1950', 69.

15. We are using the 1951 Annual Report as the 1950s Annual Report was incomplete, as recorded by the National Archives of Singapore (NAS).

16. Straits Settlements Annual Reports, 1951, R.M. I D/89, Raffles Museum and Library, 38–39, viewed at National Archives of Singapore. These jobs were randomly sampled from both the reported government and non-government daily-rated wages.

17. Hawkers Inquiry Commission, 'Report of the Hawkers Inquiry Commission, 1950', 40.

18. Hawkers Inquiry Commission, 25.

19. Hawkers Inquiry Commission, 15.

20. Tania Tze Lin Ng, 'Rendel Commission', 2009, https://eresources.nlb.gov.sg/infopedia/articles/SIP_1563_2009-09-30.html.

21. It is worth noting that of the hawker shelters named in the report, only two hawker shelters-turned-centres, Tiong Bahru (1951) and Whampoa (1952), remain today.

22. Hawkers Inquiry Commission, 'Report of the Hawkers Inquiry Commission, 1950', 17.

23. Lai, *Early Hawkers in Singapore: 1920s to 1930s*, 31.

24. Hawkers Inquiry Commission, 19.

25. The older generation often referred to hawker or hygiene inspectors as *te gu* (地牛). Singapore's *Promote Mandarin Council* explains that the term started in the 1950s — as an alert to warn (illegal) hawkers that the authorities were coming. The term itself is thought to originate from a Fujian or Chaozhou myth, either to emulate the frantic cat-and-mouse game resembled by the authorities and hawkers; or as a reference to the khaki uniforms they wore.

26. Hawkers Inquiry Commission, 'Report of the Hawkers Inquiry Commission, 1950', 16.

27. Tin Seng Lim, 'Hawkers: From Public Nuisance to National Icons', *Biblioasia*, 1 October 2013, https://biblioasia.nlb.gov.sg/vol-9/issue-3/oct-dec-2013/singapore-hawkers-national-icons/.

28. Lim.

29. The Straits Times, 'City Opens Hawker War', *The Straits Times*, 26 October 1953, Microfilm Reel NL03306.

30. Azhar Ghani, 'A Recipe for Success: How Singapore Hawker Centres Came to Be', *IPS Update* Success Matters: How Singapore Hawker Centres Came to Be (May 2011), https://lkyspp.nus.edu.sg/docs/default-source/ips/ag_history-of-hawkers_010511.pdf.

31. Nyuk Lin Yong, 'Statement by Mr. Yong Nyuk Lin, Minister for Health, at the Press Conference Held at the Administrative Headquarters of the Hawkers Department, Junction of Scotts Road with Newton Circus on Wednesday, 9th February, 1966 at 1600 Hours', 9 February 1966, 1.

Chapter 6

1. Tai Yong Tan, 'Port Cities and Hinterlands: A Comparative Study of Singapore and Calcutta', *Political Geography* 26, no. 7 (1 September 2007): 851–65, https://doi.org/10.1016/j.polgeo.2007.06.008; Tai Yong Tan,

Creating 'Greater Malaysia': Decolonization and the Politics of Merger (Singapore: ISEAS-Yusof Ishak Institute, 2008); Tai Yong Tan, *The Idea of Singapore: Smallness Unconstrained*, IPS-Nathan Lecture Series (World Scientific, 2019), https://doi.org/10.1142/11640.

2. Beng Huat Chua, *Liberalism Disavowed: Communitarianism and State Capitalism in Singapore* (Cornell University Press, 2017), 32–33, https://www.jstor.org/stable/10.7591/j.ctt1zkjz35.

3. There are no available statistics for the years between 1931 and 1947. The first post-war census was only conducted in 1947, with the relevant statistics quoted in the 1950 Hawkers Commission Inquiry.

4. Constance Turnbull, *A History of Modern Singapore, 1819–2005*, 4th ed. (National University of Singapore Press, 2020).

5. Chee Kien Lai, *Early Hawkers in Singapore: 1920s to 1930s* (Focus Publishing, 2020), 33.

6. Chua, *Liberalism Disavowed*; Turnbull, *A History of Modern Singapore, 1819–2005*.

7. Kah Seng Loh, 'The British Military Withdrawal from Singapore and the Anatomy of a Catalyst', in *Singapore in Global History*, ed. Derek Heng and Syed Muhd Khairudin Aljunied (Amsterdam University Press, 2011), 195–214, https://www.jstor.org/stable/j.ctt46mtvv.14.

8. John C. Cross, 'Co-Optation, Competition, and Resistance: State and Street Vendors in Mexico City', *Latin American Perspectives* 25, no. 2 (1998): 41–61; John Kwok, 'How Singapore's Hawker Culture Started', *TodayOnline*, 10 September 2019, https://www.todayonline.com/commentary/how-singapores-hawker-culture-started.

9. Cherian George, *Air-Conditioned Nation Revisited* (Singapore: Ethos Books, 2020), https://www.ethosbooks.com.sg/products/air-conditioned-nation-revisited; Tan, *The Idea of Singapore: Smallness Unconstrained*.

10. Hawker Policy Advisory Committee, 1974, H 063-10, Ministry of Environment/Hawkers Department (HD), 5, viewed at National Archives of Singapore.

11. Steven R. Levitsky and Lucan A. Way, 'Beyond Patronage: Violent Struggle, Ruling Party Cohesion, and Authoritarian Durability', *Perspectives on Politics* 10, no. 4 (2012): 871.

12. Dan Slater and Nicholas Rush Smith, 'The Power of Counterrevolution: Elitist Origins of Political Order in Postcolonial Asia and Africa', *American Journal of Sociology* 121, no. 5 (1 March 2016): 1480, https://doi.org/10.1086/684199.

13. Kenneth Paul Tan and Andrew Sze-Sian Tan, 'Democracy and the Grassroots Sector in Singapore', *Space and Polity* 7, no. 1 (1 April 2003): 3, https://doi.org/10.1080/13562570309245.

14. Chua, *Liberalism Disavowed*, 33–34.

15. Heng Chee Chan, *Politics in an Administration State: Where Has the Politics Gone?*, Occasional Paper / University of Singapore. Dept. of Political Science; No. 11 (Singapore: Dept. of Political Science, University of Singapore, 1975), https://www.nlb.gov.sg/biblio/4078093; Chua, *Liberalism Disavowed*.

16. Chan, *Politics in an Administration State: Where Has the Politics Gone?*

17. Singapore Parl Debates; Vol 24, Sitting No 01; Col 25; [08 December 1965].

18. Statement by Mr. Yong Nyuk Lin, Minister for Health, at the Press Conference Held at the Administrative Headquarters of the Hawkers Department, Junction of Scotts Road with Newton Circus on Wednesday, 9th February, 1966 at 1600 Hours, 09 February 1966, PressR19660209b, Ministry of Culture, 9, viewed at National Archives of Singapore.

19. Annual Report 1959–1970, Feb 1971, ENV H 098, Ministry of Environment/Hawkers Department (HD), 92, viewed at National Archives of Singapore.

20. Ministry of Environment/Hawkers Department (HD), 93.

21. Nicole Tarulevicz, *Eating Her Curries and Kway: A Cultural History of Food in Singapore* (University of Illinois Press, 2013), 34, https://www.jstor.org/stable/10.5406/j.ctt3fh59p.

22. Joshua Yeong Jia Chia and Tin Seng Lim, 'Keep Singapore Clean Campaign', 2012, https://eresources.nlb.gov.sg/infopedia/articles/SIP_2014-04-10_152216.html.

23. Kuan Yew Lee, 'Speech by the Prime Minister, Mr. Lee Kuan Yew, at the Inauguration of the "Keep Singapore Clean" Campaign on Tuesday, October 1, 1968', Press Release, 1 October 1968, National Library of Singapore.

Chapter 7

1. Jamie Han and Tin Seng Lim, 'Environmental Public Health Act', 12 May 2014, https://eresources.nlb.gov.sg/infopedia/articles/SIP_2014-05-12_133754.html.

2. Sale of Food Act (Cap 283, 1987 Rev Ed), Part III, para 20.

3. Charlotte Gill *et al.*, 'Community-Oriented Policing to Reduce Crime, Disorder and Fear and Increase Satisfaction and Legitimacy among Citizens: A Systematic Review', *Journal of Experimental Criminology* 10, no. 4 (1 December 2014): 399–428, https://doi.org/10.1007/s11292-014-9210-y; Rachel Tuffin, Julia Morris, and Alexis Poole, 'Evaluation of the Impact of the National Reassurance Policing Programme', Research Study (Home Office Research, Development and Statistics Directorate, January 2006); Paul Quinton and Julia Morris, 'Evaluation of the Impact of the National Reassurance Policing Programme', Home Office Online Report (Home Office Research, Development and Statistics Directorate, January 2006); Nadine M. Connell, Kristen Miggans, and Jean Marie McGloin, 'Can a Community Policing Initiative Reduce Serious Crime?: A Local Evaluation', *Police Quarterly* 11, no. 2 (1 June 2008): 127–50, https://doi.org/10.1177/1098611107306276.

4. The Straits Times, 'Hot Debate Expected on Expansion of Markets Dent', *The Straits Times*, 29 May 1958, Microfilm Reel NL2450.

5. 1972 Unlicensed (11,864) + 1972 Unaccounted for (19,166). See Table 7.1 and Figure 7.3.

6. Annual Report 1971–1973, Feb 1974, ENV H 098, Ministry of Environment/Hawkers Department (HD), 99, viewed at National Archives of Singapore.

7. Reorganisation of Hawker Branch, Oct 1972, FC 078, Ministry of Environment/Hawkers Department (HD), viewed at National Archives of Singapore.

8. National Archives of Singapore, 'Agency Details — Ministry of Environment/Hawkers Department (HD)', 2, accessed 19 January 2023, https://www.nas.gov.sg/archivesonline/government_records/agency-details/105.

9. Ministry of Environment/Hawkers Department (HD), 'Reorganisation of Hawker Branch', 6.

10. Annual Report 1971–1973, Feb 1974, ENV H 098, Ministry of Environment/Hawkers Department (HD), viewed at National Archives of Singapore.

11. Ministry of Environment/Hawkers Department (HD), 'Reorganisation of Hawker Branch', 11.

12. John C. Cross, 'Co-Optation, Competition, and Resistance: State and Street Vendors in Mexico City', *Latin American Perspectives* 25, no. 2 (1998): 41–61.

13. The Straits Times, 'Health Ministry Committee to Plan Hawker Centres', *The Straits Times*, 23 August 1971.

14. Hawker Policy Advisory Committee, 1974, H 063-10, Ministry of Environment/Hawkers Department (HD), 5, viewed at National Archives of Singapore.

15. Lai, *Early Hawkers in Singapore: 1920s to 1930s.*

16. Ministry of Environment/Hawkers Department (HD), 'Reorganisation of Hawker Branch', 2.

17. Ministry of Environment/Hawkers Department (HD), 'Reorganisation of Hawker Branch', 53.

18. Development of Markets and Hawker Centres, 1977, Hawkers Branch H No 810-002 File No 3, Ministry of Environment/Hawkers Department (HD), 11–12, viewed at National Archives of Singapore.

19. Ministry of Environment/Hawkers Department (HD), 'Hawker Policy Advisory Committee', 25–26.

20. Azhar Ghani, 'A Recipe for Success: How Singapore Hawker Centres Came to Be', *IPS Update* Success Matters: How Singapore Hawker Centres Came to Be (May 2011): 10, https://lkyspp.nus.edu.sg/docs/default-source/ips/ag_history-of-hawkers_010511.pdf.

21. Ghani, 10.

22. 1972 Unlicensed (11,864) + 1972 Unaccounted for (19,166).

23. Ministry of Environment/Hawkers Department (HD), 'Annual Report 1971–1973', 16.

24. There were 341 full-time employees in the Department (out of 428 authorised positions; including administrative headcount), with an additional 352 daily-rated employees (431 daily-rated employees authorised), bringing the total manpower to 693 officers.

25. Ministry of Environment/Hawkers Department (HD), 'Annual Report 1971–1973', 16.

26. Ministry of Environment/Hawkers Department (HD), 'Annual Report 1971–1973', 3.

27. Ministry of Environment/Hawkers Department (HD), 'Annual Report 1971–1973', 32.

28. Ghani, 'A Recipe for Success: How Singapore Hawker Centres Came to Be', 10.

29. Lily Kong, *Singapore Hawker Centres: People, Places, Food* (National Environment Agency, 2007), https://ink.library.smu.edu.sg/soss_research/1867/.

30. Seminar on Hawkers Policy, September 1977, H012/2, Ministry of Environment/Hawkers Department (HD), 10–11, viewed at National Archives of Singapore.

Chapter 8

1. Lily Kong, *Singapore Hawker Centres: People, Places, Food* (National Environment Agency, 2007), 19, https://ink.library.smu.edu.sg/soss_research/1867/.

2. Hawkers Inquiry Commission, 'Report of the Hawkers Inquiry Commission, 1950' (Colony of Singapore, 30 September 1950), 8, Reference Closed Collection (RCLOS), National Library of Singapore.

3. Syed Hussein Alatas, 'The Image of Indolence and the Corresponding Reality', in *The Myth of the Lazy Native* (Routledge, 1977), 70.

4. Alatas, 43.

5. Alatas, 72.

6. Alatas, 72.

7. Beng Huat Chua, 'Multiculturalism in Singapore: An Instrument of Social Control', *Race & Class* 44, no. 3 (1 January 2003): 60, https://doi.org/10.1177/0306396803044003025.

8. R. Quinn Moore, 'Multiracialism and Meritocracy: Singapore's Approach to Race and Inequality', *Review of Social Economy* 58, no. 3 (2000): 344.

9. Beng Huat Chua, *Liberalism Disavowed: Communitarianism and State Capitalism in Singapore* (NUS Press, 2017), 128.

10. Chua, 'Multiculturalism in Singapore', 60.

11. Chua, 61.
12. Siew Yeen Lim, 'Speak Mandarin Campaign', 4 July 2013, https://eresources.nlb.gov.sg/infopedia/articles/SIP_2013-07-04_122007.html.
13. Chua, 'Multiculturalism in Singapore', 71–72.
14. Jean Duruz and Cheng Khoo Gaik, *Eating Together: Food, Space, and Identity in Malaysia and Singapore* (Rowman & Littlefield Publishers, 2014), 104.
15. *A History of Singapore Hawker Culture: From Food to Architecture | Hawkers in Our Centre | Part 1/2*, 2020, https://www.youtube.com/watch?v=pw1oLexEGzo.
16. Duruz and Gaik, *Eating Together*, 103.
17. Duruz and Gaik, 32–33.
18. Duruz and Gaik, 14.
19. Singapore Parl Debates; Vol 94, Sitting No 90; Second Reading, [12 February 2019].
20. Housing & Development Board, 'HDB | Ethnic Integration Policy and SPR Quota', Housing & Development Board, 23 July 2021, https://www.hdb.gov.sg/residential/buying-a-flat/resale/eligibility/ethnic-integration-policy-and-spr-quota.
21. Government of Singapore, 'Gov.Sg | HDBs Ethnic Integration Policy Why It Still Matters', gov.sg, 13 April 2020, https://www.gov.sg/article/hdbs-ethnic-integration-policy-why-it-still-matters.
22. Robbie Goh, *Contours of Culture — Space and Social Difference in Singapore* (Hong Kong University Press, 2005), 76.
23. Singapore Parl Debates; Vol 88, Sitting No 07; Page 646; [21 November 2011].
24. Nicole Tarulevicz, *Eating Her Curries and Kway: A Cultural History of Food in Singapore*, 1st ed. (University of Illinois Press, 2013), 37.
25. Government of Singapore, 'Gov.Sg | HDBs Ethnic Integration Policy Why It Still Matters'.

Chapter 9

1. Economist Intelligence Unit, 'Worldwide Cost of Living: Singapore and Zurich Top the Ranking as the World's Most Expensive Cities', 30 November 2023, https://www.eiu.com/n/singapore-and-zurich-top-the-list-as-the-worlds-most-expensive-cities/.

2. Kay Key Teo, Hanniel Lim, and Mindy Chong, 'The Costs of Eating Out: Findings from the Makan Index 2.0', IPS Exchange Series (Lee Kuan Yew School of Public Policy, March 2023), 6.

3. Hong Yi Tay, 'Real Median Income in Singapore Falls 2.3% in 2023 on High Inflation', *The Straits Times*, 1 December 2023, https://www.straitstimes.com/singapore/jobs/real-median-income-in-singapore-falls-23-in-2023-on-high-inflation.

4. Hui Min Chew, 'Median Household Income in Singapore Rose Slightly in 2022 to S$10,099', CNA, 9 February 2023, https://www.channelnewsasia.com/singapore/real-household-income-inflation-gini-coefficient-3265036.

5. eurostat, 'How Much Do Households Spend on Food and Alcohol?', 1 February 2023, https://ec.europa.eu/eurostat/web/products-eurostat-news/w/ddn-20230201-1.

6. Statista Research Department, 'EU-27: Share of Household Expenditure for Eating Out', Statista, 3 August 2022, https://www.statista.com/statistics/1254075/eating-out-as-share-of-total-household-expenditure-in-the-european-union-by-country/.

7. Nils-Gerrit Wunsch, 'Germany: Dining out Habits 2019', Statista, 14 June 2022, https://www.statista.com/statistics/1085317/dining-out-habits-in-germany/.

8. T. B. Lund, U. Kjærnes, and L. Holm, 'Eating out in Four Nordic Countries: National Patterns and Social Stratification', *Appetite*, Eating out in modern societies: an overview of a heterogeneous habit, 119 (1 December 2017): 27, https://doi.org/10.1016/j.appet.2017.06.017.

9. Eliana Zeballos and Wilson Sinclair, 'Budget Share for Total Food Increased 13 Percent in 2022', U.S. Department of Agriculture, 19 July 2023, http://199.135.94.241/data-products/chart-gallery/gallery/chart-detail/?chartId=76967.

10. Statista Research Department, 'Frequency of Eating at Restaurants in the US 2022', Statista, 15 November 2023, https://www.statista.com/statistics/1324709/frequency-of-eating-out-at-restaurant-in-the-us/.

11. Kok Hoe Ng, You Yenn Teo, Yu Wei Neo, Ad Maulod, and Yi Ting Ting, 'What Older People Need in Singapore: A Household Budgets Study', May 2019; Kok Hoe Ng, You Yenn Teo, Yu Wei Neo, Ad Maulod, Stephanie Chok, *et al.*, 'What Older People Need in Singapore: A Household Budgets Study', 2021, https://whatsenough.sg/key-findings-mis2021/.

12. Ng, Teo, Neo, Maulod, Chok, *et al.*, 'What Older People Need in Singapore: A Household Budgets Study', 31.

13. Carol M. Devine *et al.*, 'Work Conditions and the Food Choice Coping Strategies of Employed Parents', *Journal of Nutrition Education and Behavior* 41, no. 5 (2009): 365–70, https://doi.org/10.1016/j.jneb.2009.01.007; Ming Jun Goh and Christopher Weng Wai Choong, 'Measuring Poverty: What about Eating Out?' (Khazanah Research Institute, 21 August 2020), https://www.krinstitute.org/assets/contentMS/img/template/editor/Measuring%20Poverty_What%20about%20Eating%20Out_02092020.pdf.

14. Chi Hoong Leong *et al.*, 'Examining the Cost Drivers of Hawker Food Prices' (Ministry of Trade and Industry, 26 May 2015), https://www.mti.gov.sg/Resources/feature-articles/2015/Examining-The-Cost-Drivers-of-Hawker-Food-Prices.

15. Andrew Low, 'Allow Local Hawkers a Decent Livelihood While Providing Affordable Food Options', 9 January 2020, https://www.nea.gov.sg/media/readers-letters/index/allow-local-hawkers-a-decent-livelihood-while-providing-affordable-food-options.

16. Low.

17. Low.

18. Amy Khor, 'Speech by Senior Minister of State Dr Amy Khor — Towards a Zero Waste Nation', Press Release, 2 March 2023, https://www.mse.gov.sg/resource-room/category/2023-03-02-speech-by-sms-amy-khor-at-cos-2023.

19. Belmont Lay, '10 out of 14 Stalls Quit S$40 Million Yishun Coffeeshop as Rent Set at S$10,000/Month', Mothership, 8 September 2022, https://mothership.sg/2022/09/yishun-coffeeshop-rent/.

20. Community Development Council, 'About CDC Vouchers Scheme 2021 & 2022', 3 January 2024, https://vouchers.cdc.gov.sg/about/history/.

21. Eunice Quek, 'Roast Meats Business Kay Lee Sold for $4 Million', *The Straits Times*, 21 October 2014, https://www.straitstimes.com/lifestyle/food/roast-meats-business-kay-lee-sold-for-4-million.

22. Quek.

23. Jieying Yip, 'Popular To-Ricos Kway Chap Stall Owner Looking to Retire and Sell His Recipes: "There's Nobody to Take Over"', CNA Lifestyle, 12 October 2023, https://cnalifestyle.channelnewsasia.com/dining/ricos-kwap-chap-owner-sell-recipes-372966.

24. Jieying Yip, 'Popular China Street Fritters Ngoh Hiang Stall at Maxwell Food Centre Is Closing after 81 Years', CNA Lifestyle, 24 May 2023, https://cnalifestyle.channelnewsasia.com/dining/maxwell-ngoh-hiang-china-street-fritters-closing-359766.

25. Jieying Yip, 'Maxwell's Famous China Street Fritters to Continue Operating at Telok Blangah', CNA Lifestyle, 31 August 2023, https://cnalifestyle.channelnewsasia.com/dining/china-street-fritters-telok-blangah-ngoh-hiang-formerly-maxwell-369756.

26. Beng Huat Chua, *Political Legitimacy and Housing: Singapore's Stakeholder Society* (London: Routledge, 1997), 155, https://doi.org/10.4324/9780203076187.

27. Chua, 165.

28. Kelvin E. Y. Low, 'Tasting Memories, Cooking Heritage: A Sensuous Invitation to Remember', in *Food, Foodways and Foodscapes*, World Scientific Series on Singapore's 50 Years of Nation-Building (World Scientific, 2014), 69, https://doi.org/10.1142/9789814641234_0004.

29. Lennard Yeong, 'A Day in the Life of a Third-Generation Prawn Noodle Hawker', CNA, 26 June 2018, https://www.channelnewsasia.com/lifestyle/545-whampoa-prawn-noodles-prawn-noodles-third-generation-hawker-1422596.

30. Matthew Mohan, 'In Focus: This 32-Year-Old Went from Teacher to Hawker, and Wants to Continue a Family Legacy', CNA, 6 January 2024, https://www.channelnewsasia.com/singapore/hawker-teacher-food-family-legacy-sims-vista-market-3958206?cid=telegram_cna_social_28112017_cna.

31. National Environment Agency, 'Hawkers Succession Scheme', 18 March 2022, https://www.nea.gov.sg/our-services/hawker-management/programmes-and-grants/hawkers-succession-scheme.

32. National Environment Agency, 'Hawkers' Development Programme', Hawkers' Development Programme, 13 October 2020, https://www.nea.gov.sg/our-services/hawker-management/programmes-and-grants/hawkers-development-programme.

References

🍽

A History of Singapore Hawker Culture: From Food to Architecture | Hawkers in Our Centre | Part 1/2, 2020. https://www.youtube.com/watch?v=pw1oLexEGzo.

Alatas, Syed Hussein. 'The Image of Indolence and the Corresponding Reality'. In *The Myth of the Lazy Native*. Routledge, 1977.

Alzuphar, Adolf, and Ivy Beach. 'Street Vending Is Legal in Los Angeles after a Decade of Organizing'. *Waging Nonviolence* (blog), 3 January 2019. https://wagingnonviolence.org/2019/01/street-vending-legal-los-angeles-after-decade-organizing/.

Annual Report 1959–1970, Feb 1971, ENV H 098, Ministry of Environment/Hawkers Department (HD), viewed at National Archives of Singapore.

Annual Report 1971–1973, Feb 1974, ENV H 098, Ministry of Environment/Hawkers Department (HD), viewed at National Archives of Singapore.

Bartley, W. 'Report of the Committee Appointed to Investigate the Hawker Question in Singapore'. Colonial Secretary Singapore, 4 November 1931.

Bayat, Asef. *Life as Politics: How Ordinary People Change the Middle East.* 1st edition. Stanford, Calif: Stanford University Press, 2009.

Bromley, Ray. 'Street Vending and Public Policy: A Global Review'. *International Journal of Sociology and Social Policy* 20, no. 1/2 (1 January 2000): 1–28. https://doi.org/10.1108/01443330010789052.

Cameron, John. *Our Tropical Possessions in Malayan India: Being a Descriptive Account of Singapore, Penang, Province Wellesley, and Malacca; Their Peoples,*

Products, Commerce, and Government. Smith, Elder and Co, 1865. https://eresources.nlb.gov.sg/printheritage/detail/7658c549-f1c5-47c7-b8b6-831f7eb90c58.aspx.

Chan, Heng Chee. *Politics in an Administration State: Where Has the Politics Gone?* Occasional Paper / University of Singapore. Dept. of Political Science; No. 11. Singapore: Dept. of Political Science, University of Singapore, 1975. https://www.nlb.gov.sg/biblio/4078093.

Chandran, Rina. 'Bangkok Street Vendors: From Michelin Star to Fighting Eviction'. *Reuters*, 17 September 2018, sec. Retail. https://www.reuters.com/article/us-thailand-rights-lawmaking-idUSKCN1LX23V.

Chew, Hui Min. 'Median Household Income in Singapore Rose Slightly in 2022 to S$10,099'. CNA, 9 February 2023. https://www.channelnewsasia.com/singapore/real-household-income-inflation-gini-coefficient-3265036.

Chia, Joshua Yeong Jia, and Tin Seng Lim. 'Keep Singapore Clean Campaign', 2012. https://eresources.nlb.gov.sg/infopedia/articles/SIP_2014-04-10_152216.html.

Chong, Alan. 'Introduction'. In *The Tang Shipwreck: Art and Exchange in the 9th Century*, 8–11. Asian Civilisation Museum, 2017.

Chua, Beng Huat. *Liberalism Disavowed: Communitarianism and State Capitalism in Singapore*. Cornell University Press, 2017. https://www.jstor.org/stable/10.7591/j.ctt1zkjz35.

⸻ . 'Multiculturalism in Singapore: An Instrument of Social Control'. *Race & Class* 44, no. 3 (1 January 2003): 58–77. https://doi.org/10.1177/0306396803044003025.

⸻ . *Political Legitimacy and Housing: Singapore's Stakeholder Society*. London: Routledge, 1997. https://doi.org/10.4324/9780203076187.

⸻ . 'Taking the Street Out of Street Food'. In *Food, Foodways and Foodscapes*, 23–40. World Scientific Series on Singapore's 50 Years of

Nation-Building. World Scientific, 2014. https://doi.org/10.1142/
9789814641234_0002.

Community Development Council. 'About CDC Vouchers Scheme 2021 &
2022', 3 January 2024. https://vouchers.cdc.gov.sg/about/history/.

Connell, Nadine M., Kristen Miggans, and Jean Marie McGloin. 'Can a
Community Policing Initiative Reduce Serious Crime?: A Local Evaluation'.
Police Quarterly 11, no. 2 (1 June 2008): 127–50. https://doi.org/10.1177/
1098611107306276.

Cross, John C. 'Co-Optation, Competition, and Resistance: State and Street
Vendors in Mexico City'. Latin American Perspectives 25, no. 2 (1998):
41–61.

Development of Markets and Hawker Centres, 1977, Hawkers Branch H No
810-002 File No 3, Ministry of Environment/Hawkers Department (HD),
11–12, viewed at National Archives of Singapore.

Devine, Carol M., Tracy J. Farrell, Christine E. Blake, Margaret Jastran, Elaine
Wethington, and Carole A. Bisogni. 'Work Conditions and the Food
Choice Coping Strategies of Employed Parents'. Journal of Nutrition
Education and Behavior 41, no. 5 (2009): 365–70. https://doi.
org/10.1016/j.jneb.2009.01.007.

Duruz, Jean, and Cheng Khoo Gaik. Eating Together: Food, Space, and Identity
in Malaysia and Singapore. Rowman & Littlefield Publishers, 2014.

Economist Intelligence Unit. 'Worldwide Cost of Living: Singapore and Zurich
Top the Ranking as the World's Most Expensive Cities', 30 November
2023. https://www.eiu.com/n/singapore-and-zurich-top-the-list-as-the-
worlds-most-expensive-cities/.

eurostat. 'How Much Do Households Spend on Food and Alcohol?', 1 February
2023. https://ec.europa.eu/eurostat/web/products-eurostat-news/w/ddn-
20230201-1.

Flecker, Michael. 'The Origin of the Tang Shipwreck'. In *The Tang Shipwreck: Art and Exchange in the 9th Century*, 22–39. Asian Civilisation Museum, 2017.

George, Cherian. *Air-Conditioned Nation Revisited*. Singapore: Ethos Books, 2020.

Ghani, Azhar. 'A Recipe for Success: How Singapore Hawker Centres Came to Be'. *IPS Update* Success Matters: How Singapore Hawker Centres Came to Be (May 2011). https://lkyspp.nus.edu.sg/docs/default-source/ips/ag_history-of-hawkers_010511.pdf.

Gill, Charlotte, David Weisburd, Cody W. Telep, Zoe Vitter, and Trevor Bennett. 'Community-Oriented Policing to Reduce Crime, Disorder and Fear and Increase Satisfaction and Legitimacy among Citizens: A Systematic Review'. *Journal of Experimental Criminology* 10, no. 4 (1 December 2014): 399–428. https://doi.org/10.1007/s11292-014-9210-y.

Goh, Ming Jun, and Christopher Weng Wai Choong. 'Measuring Poverty: What about Eating Out?' Khazanah Research Institute, 21 August 2020. https://www.krinstitute.org/assets/contentMS/img/template/editor/Measuring%20Poverty_What%20about%20Eating%20Out_02092020.pdf.

Goh, Robbie. *Contours of Culture — Space and Social Difference in Singapore*. Hong Kong University Press, 2005.

Government of Singapore. 'Gov.Sg | HDBs Ethnic Integration Policy Why It Still Matters'. gov.sg, 13 April 2020. https://www.gov.sg/article/hdbs-ethnic-integration-policy-why-it-still-matters.

Graaff, Kristina, and Noa Ha, eds. *Street Vending in the Neoliberal City: A Global Perspective on the Practices and Policies of a Marginalized Economy*. 1st edition. New York; Oxford: Berghahn Books, 2015.

Han, Jamie, and Tin Seng Lim. 'Environmental Public Health Act', 12 May 2014. https://eresources.nlb.gov.sg/infopedia/articles/SIP_2014-05-12_133754.html.

Hawkers Inquiry Commission. 'Report of the Hawkers Inquiry Commission, 1950'. Colony of Singapore, 30 September 1950. Reference Closed Collection (RCLOS). National Library of Singapore.

Hawker Policy Advisory Committee, 1974, H 063-10, Ministry of Environment/ Hawkers Department (HD), viewed at National Archives of Singapore.

Hays-Mitchell, Maureen. 'Streetvending in Peruvian Cities: The Spatio-Temporal Behavior of Ambulantes*'. *The Professional Geographer* 46, no. 4 (1994): 425–38. https://doi.org/10.1111/j.0033-0124.1994.00425.x.

Heng, Derek. 'Reconstructing Banzu, a Fourteenth-Century Port Settlement in Singapore'. *Journal of the Malaysian Branch of the Royal Asiatic Society* 75, no. 1 (282) (2002): 69–90.

Housing & Development Board. 'HDB | Ethnic Integration Policy and SPR Quota'. Housing & Development Board, 23 July 2021. https://www.hdb. gov.sg/residential/buying-a-flat/resale/eligibility/ethnic-integration-policy-and-spr-quota.

Jean Yip and Dawn Yip, interview by Claire Yeo, Oral History Centre, National Archives of Singapore, Accession Number 002951, Reel 1, 1 July 2005.

Khor, Amy. Press Release. 'Speech by Senior Minister of State Dr Amy Khor — Towards a Zero Waste Nation'. Press Release, 2 March 2023. https://www.mse.gov.sg/resource-room/category/2023-03-02-speech-by-sms-amy-khor-at-cos-2023.

Kong, Lily. *Singapore Hawker Centres: People, Places, Food.* National Environment Agency, 2007. https://ink.library.smu.edu.sg/soss_research/1867/.

Kuhn, Philip A. *Chinese Among Others: Emigration in Modern Times.* State and Society in East Asia. Rowman & Littlefield Publishers, 2008.

Kwok, John. 'How Singapore's Hawker Culture Started'. *TodayOnline*, 10 September 2019. https://www.todayonline.com/commentary/how-singapores-hawker-culture-started.

Lai, Ah Eng. 'The Kopitiam in Singapore: An Evolving Story about Cultural Diversity and Cultural Politics'. In *Food, Foodways and Foodscapes*, 103–32. World Scientific Series on Singapore's 50 Years of Nation-Building. World Scientific, 2014. https://doi.org/10.1142/9789814641234_0006.

Lai, Chee Kien. *Early Hawkers in Singapore: 1920s to 1930s*. Focus Publishing, 2020.

Lal, Brij V., Peter Reeves, and Rajesh Rai, eds. *The Encyclopedia of the Indian Diaspora*. Honolulu: University of Hawaii Press, 2007.

Lay, Belmont. '10 out of 14 Stalls Quit S$40 Million Yishun Coffeeshop as Rent Set at S$10,000/Month'. Mothership, 8 September 2022. https://mothership.sg/2022/09/yishun-coffeeshop-rent/.

Lee, Geok Boi. 'Wartime Victuals: Surviving the Japanese Occupation'. *Biblioasia*, 21 April 2019. https://biblioasia.nlb.gov.sg/vol-15/issue-1/apr-jun-2019/wartime-victuals/.

Lee, Kuan Yew. Press Release. 'Speech by the Prime Minister, Mr. Lee Kuan Yew, at the Inauguration of the "Keep Singapore Clean" Campaign on Tuesday, October 1, 1968'. Press Release, 1 October 1968. National Library of Singapore.

Leong, Chi Hoong, Jamie Poh, Regina Ng, Andy Fong, and Kok Kong Tan. 'Examining the Cost Drivers of Hawker Food Prices'. Ministry of Trade and Industry, 26 May 2015. https://www.mti.gov.sg/Resources/feature-articles/2015/Examining-The-Cost-Drivers-of-Hawker-Food-Prices.

Levitsky, Steven R., and Lucan A. Way. 'Beyond Patronage: Violent Struggle, Ruling Party Cohesion, and Authoritarian Durability'. *Perspectives on Politics* 10, no. 4 (2012): 869–89.

Lim, Siew Yeen. 'Speak Mandarin Campaign', 4 July 2013. https://eresources.nlb.gov.sg/infopedia/articles/SIP_2013-07-04_122007.html.

Lim, Tin Seng. 'Hawkers: From Public Nuisance to National Icons'. *Biblioasia*, 1 October 2013. https://biblioasia.nlb.gov.sg/vol-9/issue-3/oct-dec-2013/singapore-hawkers-national-icons/.

Loh, Kah Seng. 'The British Military Withdrawal from Singapore and the Anatomy of a Catalyst'. In *Singapore in Global History*, edited by Derek Heng and Syed Muhd Khairudin Aljunied, 195–214. Amsterdam University Press, 2011. https://www.jstor.org/stable/j.ctt46mtvv.14.

Low, Andrew. 'Allow Local Hawkers a Decent Livelihood While Providing Affordable Food Options', 9 January 2020. https://www.nea.gov.sg/media/readers-letters/index/allow-local-hawkers-a-decent-livelihood-while-providing-affordable-food-options.

Low, Kelvin E. Y. 'Tasting Memories, Cooking Heritage: A Sensuous Invitation to Remember'. In *Food, Foodways and Foodscapes*, 61–82. World Scientific Series on Singapore's 50 Years of Nation-Building. World Scientific, 2014. https://doi.org/10.1142/9789814641234_0004.

Lu Yaw, interview by Lu Chisen, Oral History Centre, National Archives of Singapore, Accession Number 001599, Reel 7, 4 May 1994.

Lubetkin, Mario. 'Informal Economy — Street Vending in Asia'. TerraViva, May 2006. https://www.ilo.org/wcmsp5/groups/public/---asia/---ro-bangkok/documents/publication/wcms_bk_pb_117_en.pdf.

Lund, T. B., U. Kjærnes, and L. Holm. 'Eating out in Four Nordic Countries: National Patterns and Social Stratification'. *Appetite*, Eating out in modern societies: an overview of a heterogeneous habit, 119 (1 December 2017): 23–33. https://doi.org/10.1016/j.appet.2017.06.017.

Miksic, John N. 'Ancient Singapore, Urbanism, and Commerce'. In *Singapore and the Silk Road of the Sea, 1300–1800*, 433–44. NUS Press, 2013. https://doi.org/10.2307/j.ctv1nthqk.5.

———. 'Products of Ancient Singapore'. In *Singapore and the Silk Road of the Sea, 1300–1800*, 265–87. NUS Press, 2013. https://doi.org/10.2307/j.ctv1nthqk.5.

_____ . 'Sinbad, Shipwrecks, and Singapore'. In *The Tang Shipwreck: Art and Exchange in the 9th Century*, 222–37. Asian Civilisation Museum, 2017.

_____ . *Singapore and the Silk Road of the Sea, 1300–1800*. NUS Press, 2013.

_____ . 'Temasik's Partners in Java, Thailand, Vietnam, Sri Lanka, and India'. In *Singapore and the Silk Road of the Sea, 1300–1800*, 353–66. NUS Press, 2013. https://doi.org/10.2307/j.ctv1nthqk.5.

Mohan, Matthew. 'In F: This 32-Year-Old Went from Teacher to Hawker, and Wants to Continue a Family Legacy'. CNA, 6 January 2024. https://www.channelnewsasia.com/singapore/hawker-teacher-food-family-legacy-sims-vista-market-3958206?cid=telegram_cna_social_28112017_cna.

Moore, R. Quinn. 'Multiracialism and Meritocracy: Singapore's Approach to Race and Inequality'. *Review of Social Economy* 58, no. 3 (2000): 339–60.

Murphy, Stephen A. 'Asia in the Ninth Century: The Context of the Tang Shipwreck'. In *The Tang Shipwreck: Art and Exchange in the 9th Century*, 12–21. Asian Civilisation Museum, 2017.

Murphy, Stephen A. 'Ports of Call in Ninth-Century Southeast Asia: The Route of the Tang Shipwreck'. In *The Tang Shipwreck: Art and Exchange in the 9th Century*, 238–49. Asian Civilisation Museum, 2017.

National Archives of Singapore. 'Agency Details — Ministry of Environment/Hawkers Department (HD)'. Accessed 19 January 2023. https://www.nas.gov.sg/archivesonline/government_records/agency-details/105.

National Environment Agency. 'Hawkers' Development Programme'. Hawkers' Development Programme, 13 October 2020. https://www.nea.gov.sg/our-services/hawker-management/programmes-and-grants/hawkers-development-programme.

_____ . 'Hawkers Succession Scheme', 18 March 2022. https://www.nea.gov.sg/our-services/hawker-management/programmes-and-grants/hawkers-succession-scheme.

National Heritage Board. 'The History and Evolution of Singapore's Hawker Culture'. Roots, 15 December 2021. https://www.roots.gov.sg/en/stories-landing/stories/Serving-Up-a-Legacy.

_____ . 'Former Tekka Market'. Roots, 23 June 2022. https://www.roots.gov.sg/places/places-landing/Places/landmarks/little-india-heritage-trail-serangoon-in-the-1900s/former-tekka-market.

Newbold, Thomas John. 'Political and Statistical Account of the British Settlements in the Straits of Malacca, Viz. Pinang, Malacca, and Singapore: With a History of the Malayan States on the Peninsula of Malacca', J. Murray, 1839. https://eresources.nlb.gov.sg/printheritage/detail/8123f6c8-67a1-48c6-97a6-3357c3bc5966.aspx.

Ng, Kok Hoe, You Yenn Teo, Yu Wei Neo, Ad Maulod, Stephanie Chok, and Yee Lok Wong. 'What Older People Need in Singapore: A Household Budgets Study', 2021. https://whatsenough.sg/key-findings-mis2021/.

Ng, Kok Hoe, You Yenn Teo, Yu Wei Neo, Ad Maulod, and Yi Ting Ting. 'What Older People Need in Singapore: A Household Budgets Study', May 2019.

Ng, Tania Tze Lin. 'Rendel Commission', 2009. https://eresources.nlb.gov.sg/infopedia/articles/SIP_1563_2009-09-30.html.

Quek, Eunice. 'Roast Meats Business Kay Lee Sold for $4 Million'. *The Straits Times*, 21 October 2014. https://www.straitstimes.com/lifestyle/food/roast-meats-business-kay-lee-sold-for-4-million.

Quinton, Paul, and Julia Morris. 'Evaluation of the Impact of the National Reassurance Policing Programme'. Home Office Online Report. Home Office Research, Development and Statistics Directorate, January 2006.

Reorganisation of Hawker Branch, Oct 1972, FC 078, Ministry of Environment/Hawkers Department (HD), viewed at National Archives of Singapore.

Rockhill, W. W. 'Notes on the Relations and Trade of China with the Eastern Archipelago and the Coast of the Indian Ocean during the Fourteenth Century. Part II'. *T'oung Pao* 16, no. 1 (1915): 61–159.

Sale of Food Act (Cap 283, 1987 Rev Ed), Part III, para 20.

Saw, Swee-Hock. 'Population Trends in Singapore, 1819–1967'. *Journal of Southeast Asian History* 10, no. 1 (1969): 36–49.

Seminar on Hawkers Policy, Sep 1977, H012/2, Ministry of Environment/ Hawkers Department (HD), viewed at National Archives of Singapore.

Singapore Parl Debates; Vol 24, Sitting No 01; Col 25; [08 December 1965].

———— ; Vol 88, Sitting No 07; Page 646; [21 November 2011].

———— ; Vol 94, Sitting No 90; Second Reading, [12 February 2019].

Singh, Paras. 'MCD Set to Conduct Census of Street Hawkers Operating in Delhi'. *Hindustan Times*, 21 August 2023. https://www.hindustantimes. com/cities/delhi-news/mcd-to-conduct-fresh-census-of-street-hawkers-and-vendors-in-delhi-project-expected-to-take-six-months-1016926 41479236.html.

Slater, Dan, and Nicholas Rush Smith. 'The Power of Counterrevolution: Elitist Origins of Political Order in Postcolonial Asia and Africa'. *American Journal of Sociology* 121, no. 5 (1 March 2016): 1472–1516. https://doi. org/10.1086/684199.

Soto, Hernando De. *The Other Path: The Invisible Revolution in the Third World*. 1st edition. New York: HarperCollins, 1989.

Statement by Mr. Yong Nyuk Lin, Minister for Health, at the Press Conference Held at the Administrative Headquarters of the Hawkers Department, Junction of Scotts Road with Newton Circus on Wednesday, 9th February, 1966 at 1600 Hours, 09 February 1966, PressR19660209b, Ministry of Culture, viewed at National Archives of Singapore.

Statista Research Department. 'EU-27: Share of Household Expenditure for Eating Out'. Statista, 3 August 2022. https://www.statista.com/statistics/1254075/eating-out-as-share-of-total-household-expenditure-in-the-european-union-by-country/.

———— . 'Frequency of Eating at Restaurants in the US 2022'. Statista, 15 November 2023. https://www.statista.com/statistics/1324709/frequency-of-eating-out-at-restaurant-in-the-us/.

Straits Settlements Annual Reports, 1951, R.M. I D/89, Raffles Museum and Library, 38–39, viewed at National Archives of Singapore.

Straits Settlements Blue Books, 1931, RM: I F/62, Raffles Museum and Library, 204–205, viewed at National Archives of Singapore.

Tan, Kenneth Paul, and Andrew Sze-Sian Tan. 'Democracy and the Grassroots Sector in Singapore'. *Space and Polity* 7, no. 1 (1 April 2003): 3–20. https://doi.org/10.1080/13562570309245.

Tan, Tai Yong. *Creating 'Greater Malaysia': Decolonization and the Politics of Merger*. Singapore: ISEAS-Yusof Ishak Institute, 2008.

———— . 'Port Cities and Hinterlands: A Comparative Study of Singapore and Calcutta'. *Political Geography* 26, no. 7 (1 September 2007): 851–65. https://doi.org/10.1016/j.polgeo.2007.06.008.

———— . *The Idea of Singapore: Smallness Unconstrained*. IPS-Nathan Lecture Series. WORLD SCIENTIFIC, 2019. https://doi.org/10.1142/11640.

Tarulevicz, Nicole. *Eating Her Curries and Kway: A Cultural History of Food in Singapore*. University of Illinois Press, 2013. https://www.jstor.org/stable/10.5406/j.ctt3fh59p.

Tay, Hong Yi. 'Real Median Income in Singapore Falls 2.3% in 2023 on High Inflation'. *The Straits Times*, 1 December 2023. https://www.straitstimes.com/singapore/jobs/real-median-income-in-singapore-falls-23-in-2023-on-high-inflation.

Teo, Kay Key, Hanniel Lim, and Mindy Chong. 'The Costs of Eating Out: Findings from the Makan Index 2.0'. IPS Exchange Series. Lee Kuan Yew School of Public Policy, March 2023.

The Straits Times. 'City Opens Hawker War'. *The Straits Times*, 26 October 1953. Microfilm Reel NL03306.

———. 'Health Ministry Committee to Plan Hawker Centres'. *The Straits Times*, 23 August 1971.

———. 'Hot Debate Expected on Expansion of Markets Dent.' *The Straits Times*, 29 May 1958. Microfilm Reel NL2450.

Thulaja, Naidu. 'Travelling Hawkers'. SingaporeInfopedia, 2016. https://eresources.nlb.gov.sg/infopedia/articles/SIP_47_2004-12-27.html.

Tong, Chee Kiong. 'Chinese in Singapore'. In *Encyclopedia of Diasporas: Immigrant and Refugee Cultures Around the World*, edited by Melvin Ember, Carol R. Ember, and Ian Skoggard, 723–32. Springer US, 2005. https://doi.org/10.1007/978-0-387-29904-4_75.

Tuffin, Rachel, Julia Morris, and Alexis Poole. 'Evaluation of the Impact of the National Reassurance Policing Programme'. Research Study. Home Office Research, Development and Statistics Directorate, January 2006.

Turnbull, C. M. *A History of Singapore, 1819–1988*. 2nd ed. Oxford University Press, 1989.

————— . *A History of Modern Singapore, 1819–2005*. 4th ed. National University of Singapore Press, 2020.

Vernon, Cornelius-Takahama. 'Ellenborough Market'. SingaporeInfopedia, 2005. https://eresources.nlb.gov.sg/infopedia/articles/SIP_480_2005-01-07.html.

Warren, James F. *Rickshaw Coolie: A People's History of Singapore, 1880–1940*. NUS Press, 2003.

Winstedt, R. O. 'Gold Ornaments Dug Up at Fort Canning, Singapore'. *Journal of the Malayan Branch of the Royal Asiatic Society* 6, no. 4 (105) (1928): 1–4.

Wong, Hiong Boon 黄相文, interview by Mark Wong, Oral History Centre, National Archives of Singapore, Accession Number 003526, Reel 4, 7 September 2011.

Wright, Arnold. 'Twentieth Century Impressions of British Malaya: Its History, People, Commerce, Industries, and Resources'. Lloyd's Greater Britain Publishing Company Limited, 1908. https://digital.library.cornell.edu/catalog/sea233.

Wunsch, Nils-Gerrit. 'Germany: Dining out Habits 2019'. Statista, 14 June 2022. https://wwwstatista.com/statistics/1085317/dining-out-habits-in-germany/.

UNESCO. 'Nomination File No. 01568 for Inscription in 2020 on the Representative List of the Intangible Cultural Heritage of Humanity', 19 December 2020. Nomination file No. 01568. https://ich.unesco.org/en/RL/hawker-culture-in-singapore-community-dining-and-culinary-practices-in-a-multicultural-urban-context-01568.

Yamashita, Kiyomi. 'The Residential Segregation of Chinese Dialect Groups in Singapore: With Focus on the Period before ca. 1970'. *Geographical Review of Japan* 59 (Ser. B), no. 2 (1986): 83–102.

Yatmo, Yandi Andri. 'Street Vendors as "Out of Place" Urban Elements'. *Journal of Urban Design* 13, no. 3 (1 October 2008): 387–402. https://doi.org/10.1080/13574800802320889.

Yeoh, Brenda S. A. 'The Control of "Public" Space: Conflicts over the Definition and Use of the Verandah'. In *Contesting Space in Colonial Singapore*, 243–80. Power Relations and the Urban Built Environment. NUS Press, 2003. https://doi.org/10.2307/j.ctv1ntj2v.21.

Yeong, Lennard. 'A Day in the Life of a Third-Generation Prawn Noodle Hawker'. CNA, 26 June 2018. https://www.channelnewsasia.com/lifestyle/545-whampoa-prawn-noodles-prawn-noodles-third-generation-hawker-1422596.

Yip, Jieying. 'Maxwell's Famous China Street Fritters to Continue Operating at Telok Blangah'. CNA Lifestyle, 31 August 2023. https://cnalifestyle.channelnewsasia.com/dining/china-street-fritters-telok-blangah-ngoh-hiang-formerly-maxwell-369756.

─────── . 'Popular China Street Fritters Ngoh Hiang Stall at Maxwell Food Centre Is Closing after 81 Years'. CNA Lifestyle, 24 May 2023. https://cnalifestyle.channelnewsasia.com/dining/maxwell-ngoh-hiang-china-street-fritters-closing-359766.

─────── . 'Popular To-Ricos Kway Chap Stall Owner Looking to Retire and Sell His Recipes: "There's Nobody to Take Over"'. CNA Lifestyle, 12 October 2023. https://cnalifestyle.channelnewsasia.com/dining/ricos-kwap-chap-owner-sell-recipes-372966.

Zeballos, Eliana, and Wilson Sinclair. 'Budget Share for Total Food Increased 13 Percent in 2022'. U.S. Department of Agriculture, 19 July 2023. http://199.135.94.241/data-products/chart-gallery/gallery/chart-detail/?chartId=76967.

Index

🍽